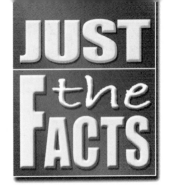

JUST the FACTS

WORLD ATLAS

By

Dee Phillips

ticktock

Copyright © ticktock Entertainment Ltd 2006
First published in Great Britain in 2006 by ticktock Media Ltd.,
Unit 2, Orchard Business Centre, North Farm Road, Tunbridge Wells, Kent, TN2 3XF
ISBN 1 86007 861 3 pbk
Printed in CHINA
A CIP catalogue record for this book is available from the British Library.

We would like to thank: Alan Grimwade and Cosmographics, Peter Bull Art Studio and Indexing Specialists (UK).

Picture credits t=top, b=bottom, c=centre, l-left, r=right
Peter Bull Art Studio: political maps, habitat maps, climate maps, locator globes. Corbis: 28, 32t, 44, 48cl, 51.
Cosmographics: physical maps. Digital Stock: 10, 11, 12, 16, 22, 23, 24, 29bl, 32, 36, 37, 43, 45, 48br, 52, 53.

Every effort has been made to trace the copyright holders, and we apologise in advance for any unintentional omissions.
We would be pleased to insert the appropriate acknowledgements in any subsequent edition of this publication.

CONTENTS

HOW TO USE THIS BOOK

JUST THE FACTS, WORLD ATLAS combines world maps with an easy-to-use way to research geography facts and find out information about the world's people, cities, countries, rivers, lakes and mountains. Each of the world's continents has its own section. In addition, you will find pages containing facts about the solar system, time zones, landforms, earthquakes, volcanoes and the oceans. For fast access to *just the facts*, follow the tips on these pages.

BOX HEADINGS
Look for heading words linked to your research to guide you to the right fact box.

CONTINENT BY CONTINENT FACTS
Each continent's section opens with two pages which show key facts and statistics about the people and geography of that continent.

TWO QUICK WAYS TO FIND A FACT:

1 Look at the detailed **CONTENTS** list on page 3 to find your topic of interest.

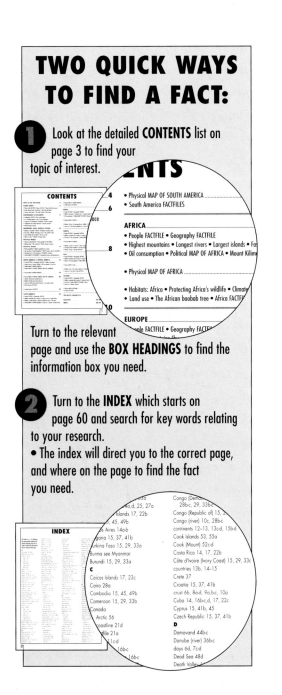

Turn to the relevant page and use the **BOX HEADINGS** to find the information box you need.

2 Turn to the **INDEX** which starts on page 60 and search for key words relating to your research.
• The index will direct you to the correct page, and where on the page to find the fact you need.

AFRICA

PEOPLE FACTFILE

Total population of continent:
887,000,000

Highest population:
Nigeria 128,771,988

Lowest population:
Djibouti 476,703

Most populous city:
Cairo, Egypt
11,146,000 residents

Average life expectancy:
Male: 51 years
Female: 53 years

Highest infant mortality rate:
Angola: 191 deaths per 1000 births – the highest in the world

• See the GLOSSARY for definitions of LIFE EXPECTANCY and INFANT MORTALITY RATE.

Average annual income per person:
Highest: Mauritius £7,200
Lowest: Sierra Leone £338

GEOGRAPHY FACTFILE

Total land area:
30,302,000 sq km

Largest country:
Sudan: 2,505,810 sq km

Smallest country:
Mayotte: 374 sq km

Largest lake:
Lake Victoria, East Africa
69,000 sq km

Largest desert:
Sahara Desert, North Africa
9,000,000 sq km
Largest desert in the world

Highest waterfall:
Tugela Falls, South Africa
Total drop: 948 m (in five steps)

• See page 33 AFRICA FACTFILES.

Africa is the second largest continent in the world. The world's biggest desert, the Sahara dominates the landscape of the north, while in the south forests and vast grasslands are home to wild animals, such as leopards, lions and elephants. The *Great Rift Valley*, one of the Earth's major geological features, runs from the Red Sea down to Mozambique. This huge crack in the Earth's surface (caused by a series of faults) is made up of mountains, volcanoes, deep valleys and lakes.

An African leopard in Samburu Game Reserve, K

HIGHEST MOUNTAINS

NAME	LOCATION	HEIGHT (metres)
Mt Kilimanjaro	Tanzania	5,895
Mt Kirinyaga (Mt Kenya)	Kenya	5,200
Mount Stanley (Margherita Peak)	Dem. Rep. Congo/Uganda	5,110
Ras Dashen	Ethiopia	4,620

LONGEST RIVERS

NAME	RIVER MOUTH	LENGTH (km)
Nile	Mediterranean	6,670
Congo	Atlantic Ocean	4,467
Niger	Atlantic Ocean	4,180
Zambezi	Indian Ocean	3,540

LARGEST ISLANDS

NAME		AREA (sq km)
Madagascar	Indian Ocean	587,040
Réunion	Indian Ocean	2,517

• See page 11 WORLD'S 10 LARGEST LAKES.

OIL CONSUMPTION

The amount of oil produced, bought and sold, and used in the world is measured in barrels. A barrel is equivalent to 192 litres.

Nigeria is Africa's largest producer of oil – 2,356,000 barrels per day

TOP 5 CONSUMERS OF OIL (USAGE PER DAY)	
Egypt	562,000 barrels
South Africa	460,000 barrels
Nigeria	275,000 barrels
Libya	216,000 barrels
Algeria	209,000 barrels

FAST FACTS

• Almost 90% of the rainfor... West Africa has been dest...

• 90% of the rainforest on t... African island of Madagas... has been destroyed. Aroun... 80% of the animal specie... found on Madagascar live... on this island and nowher... on Earth (excluding zoo populations).

• See page 24 AMAZO... RAINFOREST FACTS.

• Namibia was the first cou... the world to include prote... the environment in its constitution. Around 14%... Namibia is now protected including the entire Namib... Desert coast.

• Ancient rock paintings sho... 8000 years ago the Sahar... Desert was a lush, green... that was home to many w... animals.

• It is believed that the first... in the world to cultivate c... was Ethiopia. It was grow... the Kefa region of Ethiopi... around 1000 years ago.

28

• See page 33 AFRICA FACTFILES.

LINKS
Look for the purple links throughout the book. Each link gives details of other pages where related or additional facts can be found.

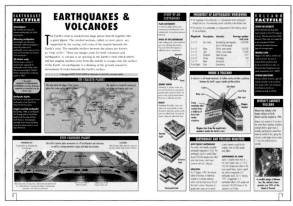

Pages packed with supplementary facts and geography information.

FACTFILES The section for each continent includes a file of information for every country.

POLITICAL MAPS

Each continent has an *at-a-glance* map which shows the territories of all the countries.

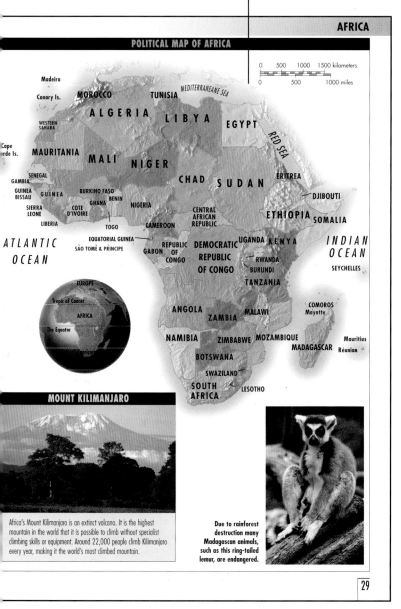

POLITICAL MAP OF AFRICA

0   500   1000   1500 kilometers
0   500   1000 miles

Madeira
Canary Is.
MOROCCO   TUNISIA   MEDITERRANEANE SEA
WESTERN SAHARA
ALGERIA   LIBYA   EGYPT
Cape Verde Is.
MAURITANIA   MALI   NIGER   CHAD   SUDAN   ERITREA   RED SEA
SENEGAL   DJIBOUTI
GAMBIA
GUINEA BISSAU   GUINEA   BURKINO FASO   BENIN   NIGERIA   CENTRAL AFRICAN REPUBLIC   ETHIOPIA   SOMALIA
SIERRA LEONE   GHANA   CAMEROON
COTE D'IVOIRE
LIBERIA   TOGO
EQUATORIAL GUINEA
SÃO TOMÉ & PRINCIPE   GABON   REPUBLIC OF CONGO   DEMOCRATIC REPUBLIC OF CONGO   UGANDA   KENYA
ATLANTIC OCEAN   RWANDA   INDIAN OCEAN
BURUNDI
SEYCHELLES
TANZANIA
EUROPE
Tropic of Cancer
AFRICA   ANGOLA   ZAMBIA   MALAWI   COMOROS   Mayotte
The Equator   NAMIBIA   ZIMBABWE   MOZAMBIQUE   Mauritius   Réunion
BOTSWANA   MADAGASCAR
SWAZILAND
SOUTH AFRICA   LESOTHO

MOUNT KILIMANJARO

Africa's Mount Kilimanjaro is an extinct volcano. It is the highest mountain in the world that it is possible to climb without specialist climbing skills or equipment. Around 22,000 people climb Kilimanjaro every year, making it the world's most climbed mountain.

Due to rainforest destruction many Madagascan animals, such as this ring-tailed lemur, are endangered.

29

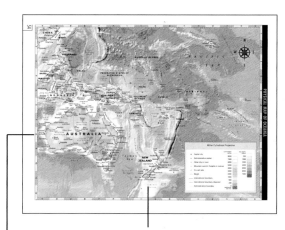

PHYSICAL MAPS

Each continent has a detailed physical map which shows:

- Borders
- Capital cities
- Major cities
- Highest mountains
- Rivers and lakes
- Land heights above and below sea level
- Oceans, seas and major bodies of water

HOW TO FIND A PLACE USING THE PHYSICAL MAPS

Look up the place you want to find in the MAP INDEX which begins on page 62. There you will see a page number and a letter/number code (for example 38 H5). Look for the letter and number on the grid at the edge of the relevant page. Follow the two tracks. You will find the place you are looking for where the two tracks meet.

GLOSSARY

A GLOSSARY of words and terms used in this book begins on page 58.

The glossary provides additional information to supplement the facts on the main pages.

JUST THE FACTS

Each topic box presents the facts you need in lists; short, quick-to-read bullet points; charts and tables.

PLANET EARTH FACTFILE

Age of the Earth:
4.5 billion years old

Diameter at the Equator:
12,756 km across

Diameter at the Poles:
12,714 km across

Circumference at the Equator:
38,024 km around

Weight (mass) of the Earth:
6.6 sextillion tonnes

Average surface temperature:
15°C (59°F)

Rotational speed at the Equator:
1,600 km/h
The Earth is a ball spinning on an axis, so places at the Equator (the centre) spin much faster than at the North and South Poles.

MOON FACTFILE

A moon is a ball of rock which orbits a planet. Moons are sometimes called satellites. The Earth has one moon.

Length of the Moon's orbit:
The Moon orbits the Earth once every 27 days, 7 hours and 43 minutes. It takes the same length of time to rotate once on its own axis.

Orbiting speed:
3,700 km/h

Distance from the Earth:
The distance varies from 356,399 to 384,403 km.

Circumference of the Moon:
10,927 km around the middle

Our planet, which we call the Earth, is a ball of rock travelling through space at around 108,000 kilometres an hour. The Earth is moving around a star, which we call the Sun. The pulling power, or gravity, of the Sun keeps the Earth on an oval-shaped course. The time it takes the Earth to make one complete orbit of the Sun is called a year.

The Earth is one of nine planets that make up the Solar System.

PLANET EARTH FROM SPACE

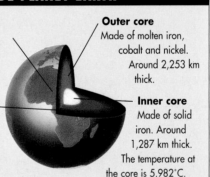

When viewed from space the Earth looks blue, brown and white.

The vast areas of blue are oceans – 70.7% of the Earth's surface is covered in water: an area of 360,000,000 sq km.

The brown areas are landmasses – 29.3% of the Earth's surface is dry land: an area of 149,450,000 sq km.

The white areas are clouds hanging in the atmosphere (the layer of gases surrounding the Earth).

INSIDE PLANET EARTH

The crust
Thickness varies from 4.5 km (beneath the oceans) to 19 to 69 km (where there are landmasses and mountains).

The mantle
Made of magnesium and silicon. Around 2,897 km thick. About 100 km down, the mantle becomes molten (melted).

Outer core
Made of molten iron, cobalt and nickel. Around 2,253 km thick.

Inner core
Made of solid iron. Around 1,287 km thick. The temperature at the core is 5,982°C.

EARTH TIME

A year
The exact time it takes for the Earth to make one complete orbit of the Sun is 365 days, 6 hours, 9 minutes and 10 seconds.

A leap year
Because it is more convenient to use a calendar of 365 whole days, every four years we have to add up the extra 6 hours, 9 minutes and 10 seconds to make an extra day. These 366-day years are called leap years.

A day
As the Earth orbits the Sun it also rotates, or spins around. One complete rotation takes 23 hours, 56 minutes and 4 seconds. We round this period up to 24 hours and call it a day.

HOT AND COLD PLANET

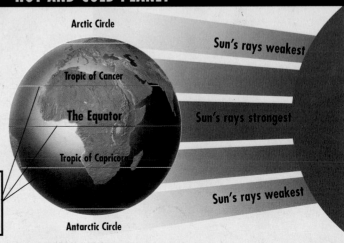

Because the Earth is curved like a ball, the Sun's rays are weaker and more spread out at the Arctic and Antarctic making these regions cold.

At the Equator the Sun's rays are the most concentrated, so this region is very hot.

In order to measure the Earth and to help us find places and talk about different regions, we divide up the Earth using imaginary lines.

Arctic Circle

Tropic of Cancer

The Equator

Tropic of Capricorn

Antarctic Circle

Sun's rays weakest

Sun's rays strongest

Sun's rays weakest

SUMMER AND WINTER

As the Earth spins it also tilts, so its position in relation to the Sun gradually changes throughout the year.

When the northern hemisphere (the region above the Equator) is tilted towards the Sun, countries in the north have summer. Countries in the southern hemisphere have winter.

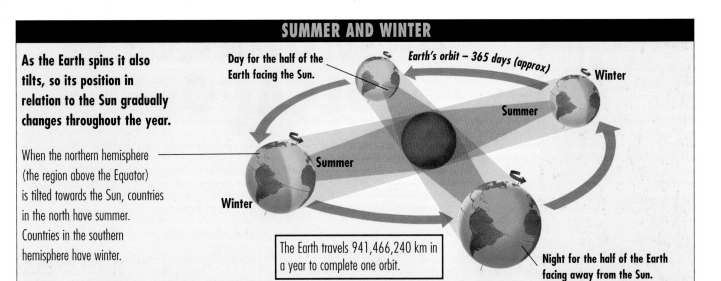

Day for the half of the Earth facing the Sun.

Earth's orbit – 365 days (approx)

Winter

Summer

Summer

Winter

The Earth travels 941,466,240 km in a year to complete one orbit.

Night for the half of the Earth facing away from the Sun.

THE SOLAR SYSTEM

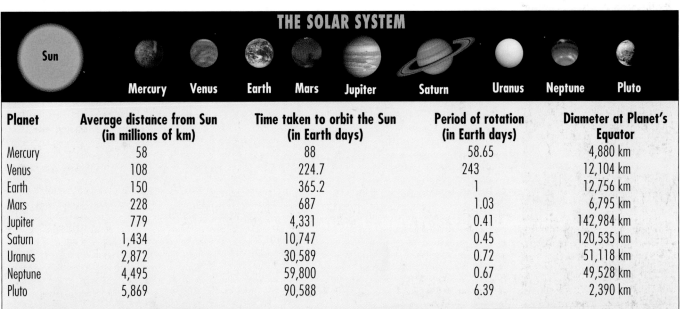

Sun

Mercury Venus Earth Mars Jupiter Saturn Uranus Neptune Pluto

Planet	Average distance from Sun (in millions of km)	Time taken to orbit the Sun (in Earth days)	Period of rotation (in Earth days)	Diameter at Planet's Equator
Mercury	58	88	58.65	4,880 km
Venus	108	224.7	243	12,104 km
Earth	150	365.2	1	12,756 km
Mars	228	687	1.03	6,795 km
Jupiter	779	4,331	0.41	142,984 km
Saturn	1,434	10,747	0.45	120,535 km
Uranus	2,872	30,589	0.72	51,118 km
Neptune	4,495	59,800	0.67	49,528 km
Pluto	5,869	90,588	6.39	2,390 km

TIME ZONES

As the Earth spins, some parts of the world are in sunlight while others are in darkness so it cannot be the same time everywhere.

Therefore the world has been divided up into 24 time zones. Because the Earth rotates through 360 degrees every 24 hours, each time zone covers 15 degrees of longitude on a map of the world.

The zero point of longitude is at Greenwich in London. It is known as the *Greenwich meridian*. As you move east or west from Greenwich through each new time zone, you add or subtract an hour of time.

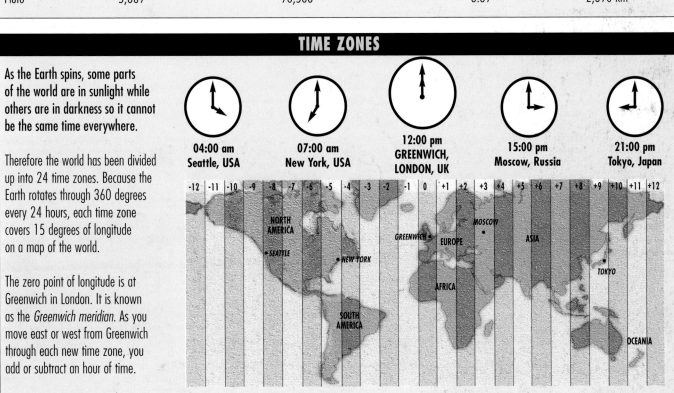

04:00 am
Seattle, USA

07:00 am
New York, USA

12:00 pm
GREENWICH,
LONDON, UK

15:00 pm
Moscow, Russia

21:00 pm
Tokyo, Japan

-12 -11 -10 -9 -8 -7 -6 -5 -4 -3 -2 -1 0 +1 +2 +3 +4 +5 +6 +7 +8 +9 +10 +11 +12

NORTH AMERICA
SEATTLE
NEW YORK
SOUTH AMERICA
GREENWICH
EUROPE
AFRICA
MOSCOW
ASIA
TOKYO
OCEANIA

EARTHQUAKES & VOLCANOES

The Earth's crust is cracked into huge pieces that fit together like a giant jigsaw. The cracked sections, called *tectonic plates*, are supported by the oozing, soft rocks of the mantle beneath the Earth's crust. The unstable borders between the plates are known as *'rings of fire'*. These are danger zones for both volcanoes and earthquakes. A volcano is an opening in the Earth's crust which allows red-hot magma (molten rock) from the mantle to escape onto the surface of the Earth. An earthquake is a shaking of the ground caused by movements of rocks beneath the Earth's surface.

• See page 6 INSIDE PLANET EARTH for information on the Earth's crust and mantle.

THE CRACKED PLANET

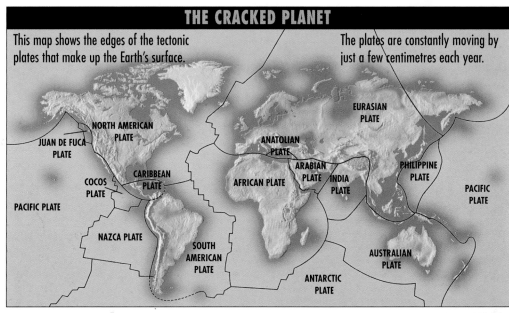

This map shows the edges of the tectonic plates that make up the Earth's surface.

The plates are constantly moving by just a few centimetres each year.

NORTH AMERICAN PLATE
JUAN DE FUCA PLATE
COCOS PLATE
CARIBBEAN PLATE
PACIFIC PLATE
NAZCA PLATE
SOUTH AMERICAN PLATE
AFRICAN PLATE
ANATOLIAN PLATE
ARABIAN PLATE
INDIA PLATE
EURASIAN PLATE
PHILIPPINE PLATE
PACIFIC PLATE
AUSTRALIAN PLATE
ANTARCTIC PLATE

EVER-CHANGING PLANET

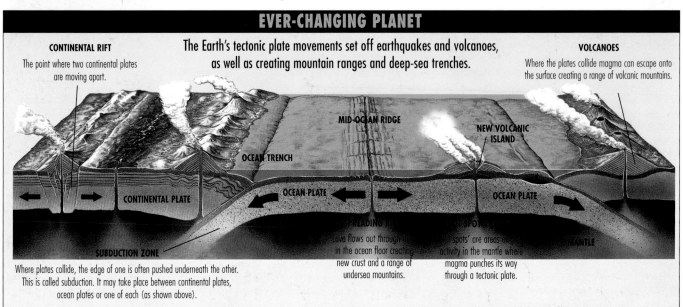

The Earth's tectonic plate movements set off earthquakes and volcanoes, as well as creating mountain ranges and deep-sea trenches.

CONTINENTAL RIFT
The point where two continental plates are moving apart.

VOLCANOES
Where the plates collide magma can escape onto the surface creating a range of volcanic mountains.

MID-OCEAN RIDGE
NEW VOLCANIC ISLAND
OCEAN TRENCH
CONTINENTAL PLATE
OCEAN PLATE
OCEAN PLATE

SPREADING RIDGE
Lava flows out through the ocean floor creating new crust and a range of undersea mountains.

HOT SPOT
'Hot spots' are areas of activity in the mantle where magma punches its way through a tectonic plate.

MANTLE

SUBDUCTION ZONE
Where plates collide, the edge of one is often pushed underneath the other. This is called subduction. It may take place between continental plates, ocean plates or one of each (as shown above).

STORY OF AN EARTHQUAKE

PLATE MOVEMENTS
Two tectonic plates slowly move, squeezing and stretching the rocks underground. An enormous pressure builds up.

FOCUS OF THE EARTHQUAKE
Miles underground, rocks break and give way releasing the pressure. The point where this happens is called the *focus* or *hypocentre*.

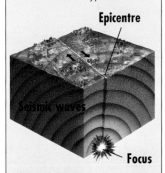

Epicentre

Seismic waves

Focus

SEISMIC WAVES
Vibrations, or *seismic waves*, are sent out from the focus causing the ground at the surface to shake. The point on the surface directly above the focus is called the *epicentre*.

FAULTS
Sometimes the Earth's crust is put under such pressure that it cracks. The places where the surface cracks open are called *faults*. The lines the cracks create are called *fault lines*.

Normal fault

Reverse fault

Horizontal fault

FREQUENCY OF EARTHQUAKES WORLDWIDE

- The magnitude of an earthquake is a measurement of the earthquake's strength and size. The measuring system used here is the *Richter Scale*.

- The intensity of an earthquake is a measurement of the shaking caused by the earthquake.

Magnitude	Description	Intensity	Average number each year
2 to 2.9	Very minor	Recorded by seismographs, but not felt by people	1,300,000
3 to 3.9	Minor	Felt by some people	130,000
4 to 4.9	Light	Felt by many people	13,000
5 to 5.9	Moderate	Slight damage	1319
6 to 6.9	Strong	Damaging	134
7 to 7.9	Major	Destructive	17
8 and higher	Great	Devastating	1

INSIDE A VOLCANO

A volcano is a self-made mountain. Its hollow centre provides a pathway between the Earth's upper mantle and the surface.

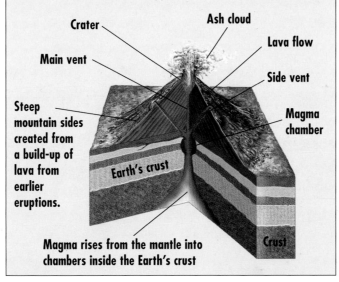

Crater

Ash cloud

Main vent

Lava flow

Side vent

Steep mountain sides created from a build-up of lava from earlier eruptions.

Magma chamber

Earth's crust

Crust

Magma rises from the mantle into chambers inside the Earth's crust

EARTHQUAKE AND VOLCANO DISASTERS

MOST DEADLY EARTHQUAKE
The world's most deadly, recorded earthquake happened in 1556. The earthquake struck in central China. Around 830,000 people were killed when their homes, which were carved in soft rock, collapsed.

KRAKATOA
On 27 August, 1883, the volcanic island of Krakatoa, in Indonesia, erupted in a massive explosion which could be heard across 8% of the Earth's surface. Thousands of people were swept out to sea by a giant tsunami caused by the eruption. Over 36,000 people were killed.

EARTHQUAKES IN JAPAN
Japan is situated where four of the Earth's plates meet. In 1923, 143,000 people were killed in the area around Tokyo, Japan's capital city, when a magnitude—8.3 earthquake struck. On 17 January, 1995, a magnitude—7.2 earthquake killed 5,500 people and destroyed 100,000 homes in the Japanese city of Kobe.

VOLCANO FACTFILE

ACTIVE OR EXTINCT?
Active volcanoes are those that erupt regularly or have the capacity to erupt. They are sometimes called dormant if they have not erupted for a very long period. Extinct volcanoes are dead volcanoes, they will not erupt again.

MAGMA/LAVA
Magma is the red-hot, melted rock inside a volcano. As soon as magma leaves a volcano and bursts out into the air or sea, it is known as lava. Erupting lava can reach temperatures of to 1,200°C.

PLINIAN ERUPTIONS
During a 'plinian eruption', gas-rich magma explodes inside a volcano. This causes cinders, ash and gases to be fired up into the air – sometimes as high as 30 km!

WORLD'S LARGEST VOLCANO

Mauna Loa, Hawaii, is the largest volcano on Earth. Mauna Loa last erupted in 1984.

Mauna Loa's summit is 9 km from the ocean floor. However, scientists estimate that its great mass is actually squashing the ocean floor down by another 8 km, giving the volcano a total height of just under 17 km from seafloor base to summit.

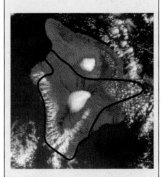

A satellite image of Mauna Loa. The volcano's base spreads over 50% of the island of Hawaii.

MOUNTAINS, LAKES, RIVERS & OCEANS

Mountains are formed when the Earth's tectonic plates move.

- As layers of rocks push against each other, they buckle and fold at the edges. Mountains are pushed up at upfolds, and valleys are formed in downfolds.

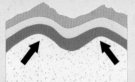

Fold mountain

- When the Earth's crust cracks on a fault, layers of rock on one side of the crack can be pushed up to form a mountain.

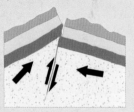

Fault mountain

- When molten magma bursts through the Earth's crust it hardens and cools, sometimes forming a mountain.

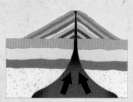

Volcanic mountain

- Heat from molten rock in the mantle pushes layers of solid rock in the Earth's crust upward creating a bulge on the Earth's surface.

Dome mountain

• See page 8
THE CRACKED PLANET and
EVER-CHANGING PLANET.

From the Himalayas, the world's tallest mountains, to the deepest ocean trench over 10 kilometres below the surface of the Pacific ocean, the Earth's surface is slowly, but surely changing. Mountains grow centimetre by centimetre year by year, rivers carve new channels as they rush to the sea, and oceans push and pull at the edges of the land.

WORLD'S 10 HIGHEST MOUNTAIN PEAKS

Some mountain peaks stand alone high above the surrounding landscape, but most mountains are joined together to form a *range*. When several ranges of mountains are grouped together, they are called a *chain*.

The world's ten highest mountain peaks are all in the same range of mountains in Asia — the Himalayas.

Mountain name	Country	Height (metres)
1. Everest	China/Nepal	8,850
2. K2	China/Pakistan	8,611
3. Kanchenjunga	India/Nepal	8,586
4. Lhotse	China/Nepal	8,516
5. Makalu	China/Nepal	8,481
6. Cho Oyu	China/Nepal	8,201
7. Dhaulagiri	Nepal	8,172
8. Manaslu	Nepal	8,156
9. Nanga Parbat	Pakistan	8,126
10. Annapurna	Nepal	8,078

Mount Everest — the highest mountain in the world.

THE ANDES

- The Andes are the world's longest chain of mountains. They stretch down the west coast of South America for around 8,800 km.

- The Andes include the highest mountain in South America, Aconcagua, in Argentina, which is 6,960 m high. Many of the mountains in the Andes are volcanic.

- The Andes were formed around 70 million years ago by the collision of the Nazca Oceanic Plate with the South American Continental Plate.

WORLD'S 10 LONGEST RIVERS

Rivers begin their lives as small streams high up mountains or hills. They grow and grow, joining with other small rivers, until they form one big river which reaches the sea or a lake. River water comes from rainfall, melted ice or snow, or groundwater from inside the Earth's crust.

River		Length (km)
1. Nile	Africa	6,670
2. Amazon	South America	6,450
3. Yangtze	Asia	6,380
4. Mississippi-Missouri	N. America	6,020
5. Yenisey-Angara	Asia	5,550
6. Huang He (Yellow)	Asia	5,464
7. Ob-Irtysh	Asia	5,410
8. Congo	Africa	4,667
9. Parana	South America	4,500
10. Mekong	Asia	4,350

(The figures are rounded as appropriate.)

The River Nile snakes through Egypt's capital city, Cairo. The Nile flows through northeast Africa out into the Mediterranean Sea.

THE WORLD'S OCEANS

There are five oceans in the world and many smaller seas within the oceans.

The Pacific Ocean is the world's largest ocean — its total area is greater than the amount of dry land on Earth.

The Southern Ocean circumnavigates the continent of Antarctica. It officially became an ocean in 2000, and was formed from the southern sections of the Atlantic, Indian and Pacific oceans.

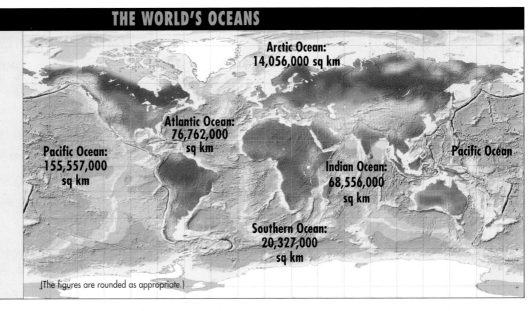

Arctic Ocean:
14,056,000 sq km

Atlantic Ocean:
76,762,000 sq km

Pacific Ocean:
155,557,000 sq km

Indian Ocean:
68,556,000 sq km

Pacific Ocean

Southern Ocean:
20,327,000 sq km

(The figures are rounded as appropriate.)

OCEAN DEPTHS AND COASTLINES

The deepest points in each of the world's oceans are listed below. They are measured from *sea level* (the surface of the ocean).

Challenger Deep in the Mariana Trench	Pacific Ocean	−10,924 m
Milwaukee Deep, Puerto Rico Trench	Atlantic Ocean	−8,605 m
Java Trench	Indian Ocean	−7,258 m
Southern end of South Sandwich Trench	Southern Ocean	−7,235 m
Fram Basin	Arctic Ocean	−4,665 m

• See page 8
EVER-CHANGING PLANET
for information on how ocean trenches are formed.

Total length of coastline on each ocean:

Pacific Ocean	135,663 km
Atlantic Ocean	111,866 km
Indian Ocean	66,526 km
Arctic Ocean	45,389 km
Southern Ocean	17,968 km

Coasts can be icy, rocky or sandy, like these beaches at Rio de Janeiro, Brazil, on South America's east coast.

OCEAN CURRENTS

The oceans are never still. Tides rise and fall, and ocean currents, which are rather like ocean rivers, move the water around.

→ **Warm water currents**
→ **Cold water currents**

Surface currents are created by the wind. Currents deep underwater are created by temperature differences and the amount of salt in the water.

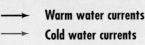

WHAT IS A LAKE?

A lake is a large body of water surrounded by land. Most lakes are full of fresh water. Lakes form in basins (hollows) in the Earth's surface. Rainwater or melted snow and ice collect in the basin. Water also feeds in from rivers and streams.

• Lakes without a river flowing outwards lose water through evaporation. The water becomes salty as minerals in the lake become more concentrated. The world's largest lake, the Caspian Sea, is a salt water lake.

• Lake Baykal in Russia is the world's deepest lake. Its deepest point is 1,620 m deep.

WORLD'S 10 LARGEST LAKES

Lake		Area (sq km)
1. Caspian Sea	Asia	371,000
2. Lake Superior	Canada/USA	82,000
3. Lake Victoria	East Africa	69,000
4. Lake Huron	Canada/USA	59,600
5. Lake Michigan	USA	57,800
6. Lake Tanganyika	Central Africa	33,000
7. Great Bear Lake	Canada	31,300
8. Lake Baykal	Russia	31,000
9. Lake Malawi/Nyasa	East Africa	29,600
10. Aral Sea	Kazakhstan/Uzbekistan	28,687

(The figures are rounded as appropriate.)

Lake Victoria is the largest lake in Africa. Over 200 species of fish live in its waters.

Total surface area of Earth:
509,450,000 sq km

Total length of coastline on Earth:
356,000 km

Largest ocean:
Pacific Ocean
Total area: 155,557,000 sq km

Largest oceanic island:
Greenland, North America
Total area: 2,166,086 sq km

Largest lake:
Caspian Sea, Asia
A land-locked salt water lake.
Total area: 371,000 sq km

Largest freshwater lake:
Lake Superior, Canada/USA
Total area: 82,000 sq km

Largest freshwater island:
Ilha de Marajó, Brazil, South America. An island at the mouth of the Amazon River.
Total area: 40,145 sq km

Longest river:
Nile, Africa
Total length: 6,670 km

Tallest mountain:
Mount Everest, Himalayas range, border of China and Nepal, Asia
Height: 8,850 m

Longest cave system:
Mammoth Caves, USA
580 km of caves have been explored and mapped.

Largest gorge:
Grand Canyon, USA
Total length: 446 km
Widest point: 24 km

Largest desert:
Sahara desert, North Africa
Total area: 9,000,000 sq km

Highest waterfall:
Angel Falls, Venezuela, South America, has an uninterrupted fall of 979 m of water.

Hottest recorded temperature:
At Al Aziziyah, Libya
58°C

Lowest recorded temperature:
Vostok Base, Antarctica
−53°C

PHYSICAL WORLD

Planet Earth is three dimensional: it has length, breadth and height. In order to create two dimensional maps for an atlas, cartographers (map makers) have devised ways to convert the Earth's curved surface into flat images, called *projections*. The projection below is a physical map of the whole world. It shows physical features such as mountains, and has a key that shows how the map's colours denote different environments, such as tundra and desert.

PHYSICAL MAP OF THE WORLD

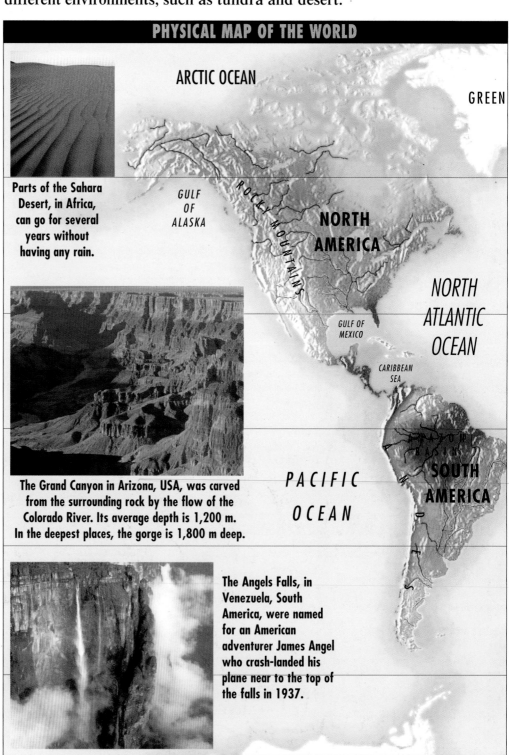

ARCTIC OCEAN

GREEN

Parts of the Sahara Desert, in Africa, can go for several years without having any rain.

GULF OF ALASKA

ROCKY MOUNTAINS

NORTH AMERICA

NORTH ATLANTIC OCEAN

GULF OF MEXICO

CARIBBEAN SEA

AMAZON BASIN

SOUTH AMERICA

PACIFIC OCEAN

The Grand Canyon in Arizona, USA, was carved from the surrounding rock by the flow of the Colorado River. Its average depth is 1,200 m. In the deepest places, the gorge is 1,800 m deep.

The Angels Falls, in Venezuela, South America, were named for an American adventurer James Angel who crash-landed his plane near to the top of the falls in 1937.

MAKING MAPS

The projection on these pages was created by a process that was a bit like peeling an orange, then smoothing the skin out!

The flat, peeled version of the Earth was stretched and manipulated by computer to create the map we see below.

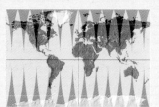

THE CONTINENTS

CONTINENT	Area (sq km)	Percentage of total land
Asia	44,500,000	29.8%
Africa	30,302,000	20.3%
North and Central America	24,241,000	16.2%
South America	17,793,000	11.9%
Antarctica	14,100,000	9.4%
Europe	9,957,000	6.7%
Oceania	8,557,000	5.7%

PHYSICAL MAP OF THE WORLD

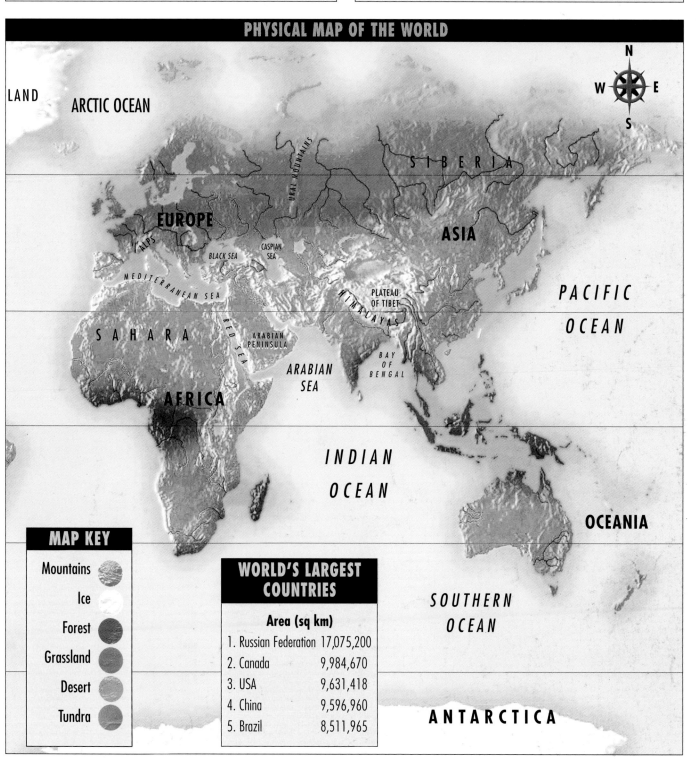

LAND

ARCTIC OCEAN

SIBERIA

EUROPE

URAL MOUNTAINS

ASIA

ALPS

BLACK SEA

CASPIAN SEA

MEDITERRANEAN SEA

PLATEAU OF TIBET

PACIFIC OCEAN

SAHARA

RED SEA

ARABIAN PENINSULA

HIMALAYAS

ARABIAN SEA

BAY OF BENGAL

AFRICA

INDIAN OCEAN

OCEANIA

SOUTHERN OCEAN

ANTARCTICA

MAP KEY

- Mountains
- Ice
- Forest
- Grassland
- Desert
- Tundra

WORLD'S LARGEST COUNTRIES

	Area (sq km)
1. Russian Federation	17,075,200
2. Canada	9,984,670
3. USA	9,631,418
4. China	9,596,960
5. Brazil	8,511,965

POLITICAL WORLD

This map is a political map of the world. The colours on the map show how people divide up the world into territories, or individual countries. The number of countries in the world changes often. Sometimes large countries divide up into smaller countries, or a group of small countries will join together to become one large country.

If you were to look at a political map of the world 50 years from now, it might look quite different to how the political world looks today.

HIGHEST POPULATION BY COUNTRY

1.	China	1,306,313,812
2.	India	1,080,264,388
3.	USA	295,734,134
4.	Indonesia	241,973,879
5.	Brazil	186,112,794
6.	Pakistan	162,419,946
7.	Bangladesh	144,319,628
8.	Russian Fed.	143,420,309
9.	Nigeria	128,771,988
10.	Japan	127,417,244

AGE STRUCTURE OF WORLD POPULATION

MEDIAN AGE is the age that divides a population in two – half the people are younger than this age, and half are older.

This chart shows the world's population by age group.

65+ years: 7.3%
0–14 years: 27.8%
15–64 years: 64.9%

Total world population	
median age:	27.6 years
Male:	27 years
Female:	28.2 years

WORLD'S LARGEST CITIES BY POPULATION

1.	Tokyo	Japan	35,327,000
2.	Mexico City	Mexico	19,013,000
3.	New York	USA	18,498,000
4.	Mumbai (Bombay)	India	18,336,000
5.	São Paulo	Brazil	18,333,000
6.	Delhi	India	15,334,000
7.	Kolkata (Calcutta)	India	14,299,000
8.	Buenos Aires	Argentina	13,349,000
9.	Jakarta	Indonesia	13,194,000
10.	Shanghai	China	12,665,000
27.	London	UK	7,615,000

(All figures include the city centre and surrounding urban areas.)

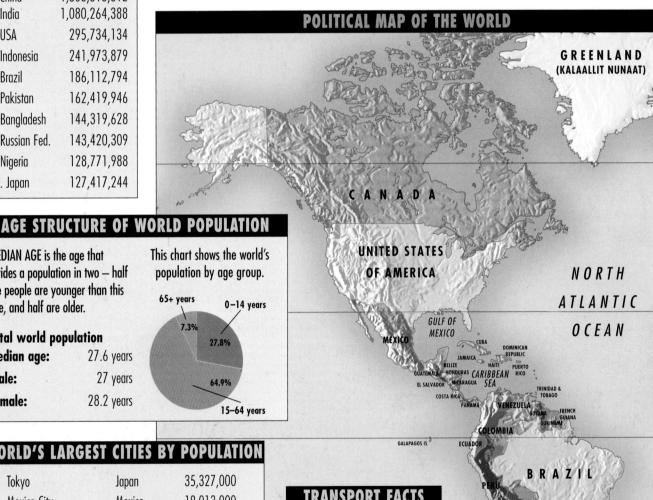

POLITICAL MAP OF THE WORLD

GREENLAND
(KALAALLIT NUNAAT)

CANADA

UNITED STATES
OF AMERICA

NORTH
ATLANTIC
OCEAN

GULF OF
MEXICO

MEXICO

CUBA

DOMINICAN
REPUBLIC

JAMAICA

BELIZE
HAITI
PUERTO
RICO

GUATEMALA HONDURAS CARIBBEAN
SEA

EL SALVADOR NICARAGUA

TRINIDAD &
TOBAGO

COSTA RICA

PANAMA VENEZUELA

GUYANA FRENCH
GUIANA

SURINAME

COLOMBIA

GALAPAGOS IS ECUADOR

BRAZIL

PERU

PARAGUAY

URUGUAY

ARGENTINA

CHILE

FALKLAND/MALVINAS ISLANDS

TRANSPORT FACTS

**Total length of roads
in the world:**
32,345,165 km

**Total length of railway
in the world:**
1,115,205 km

**Number of airports
in the world:**
49,973

LIFE EXPECTANCY

Average life expectancy at birth total population:
Male: 63 years
Female: 66 years

Highest life expectancy:
Andorra, Europe 83.5 years

Lowest life expectancy:
Botswana, Africa 34 years

• See the GLOSSARY for a definition of life expectancy.

WEALTH BY CONTINENT

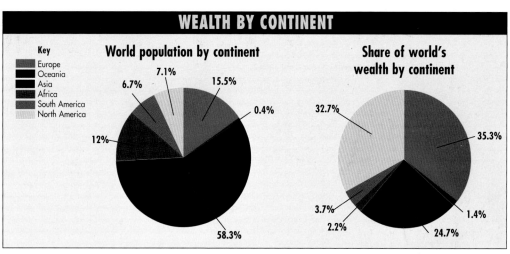

Key
- Europe
- Oceania
- Asia
- Africa
- South America
- North America

World population by continent
7.1%
6.7%
15.5%
0.4%
12%
58.3%

Share of world's wealth by continent
32.7%
35.3%
3.7%
2.2%
1.4%
24.7%

POLITICAL MAP OF THE WORLD

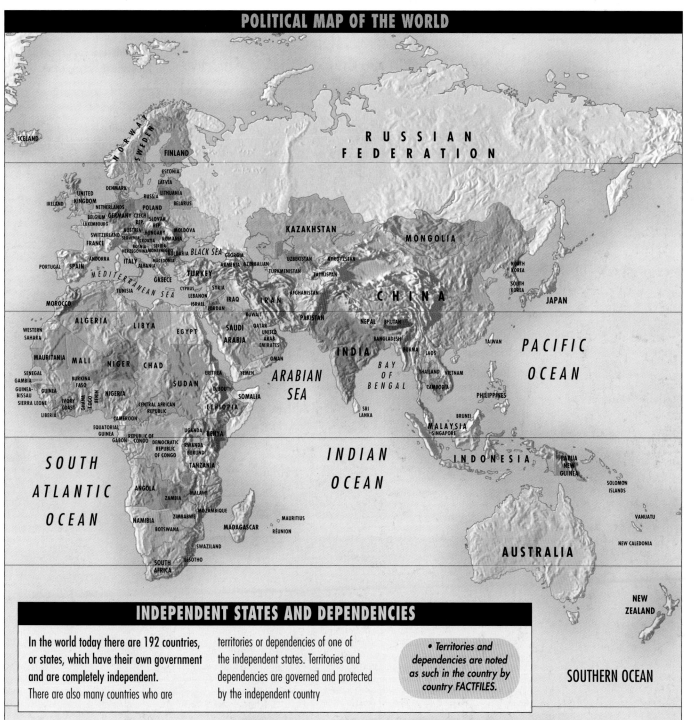

INDEPENDENT STATES AND DEPENDENCIES

In the world today there are 192 countries, or states, which have their own government and are completely independent.
There are also many countries who are territories or dependencies of one of the independent states. Territories and dependencies are governed and protected by the independent country

• Territories and dependencies are noted as such in the country by country FACTFILES.

• See the GLOSSARY for definitions of LIFE EXPECTANCY and INFANT MORTALITY RATE.

Average annual income per person:
Highest: USA £22,500
Lowest: Haiti £850

GEOGRAPHY FACTFILE

Total land area:
24,241,000 sq km

Largest country:
Canada: 9,984,670 sq km
Canada is the second largest country in the world

Smallest country:
Bermuda: 53.3 sq km

Largest lake:
Lake Superior, Canada/USA
Total area: 82,000 sq km

Largest desert:
Great Basin Desert, USA
Total area: 490,000 sq km

Highest waterfall:
Ribbon Fall, Yosemite National Park, USA
Total drop: 491 m

• See page 21 NORTH AMERICA FACTFILES and page 22 CENTRAL AMERICA FACTFILES.

The North American continent lies between the Atlantic and Pacific Oceans. This varied region stretches from the icy plains of Arctic North America to the hot deserts and lush tropical forests of Central America and the Caribbean islands. Dominating western North America are the Rocky Mountains, or *Rockies*, which stretch for 4,800 kilometres from Canada to New Mexico in the United States of America.

Rising majestically from the desert floor, 300-metre high sandstone rock forms in Monument Valley, Utah, USA.

HIGHEST MOUNTAINS

NAME	LOCATION	HEIGHT (metres)
Mt McKinley	USA (Alaska)	6,194
Mt Logan	Canada	6,050
Pico de Orizaba	Mexico	5,610
Mt St Elias	USA/Canada	5,489

LONGEST RIVERS

NAME	RIVER MOUTH	LENGTH (km)
Mississippi-Missouri	Gulf of Mexico	6,020
Mackenzie	Arctic Ocean	4,241
Yukon	Pacific Ocean	3,185
Rio Grande	Gulf of Mexico	3,040

LARGEST ISLANDS

NAME		AREA (sq km)
Greenland	Atlantic Ocean	2,166,086
Baffin Island	Canada	507,897
Victoria Island	Canada	212,120

• See page 11 WORLD'S 10 LARGEST LAKES.

OIL CONSUMPTION

Oil is a fossil fuel (a natural resource) which we burn to produce power for heating and lighting. It is also used as fuel for cars, lorries and planes.

Oil production and consumption is measured in barrels. A barrel is equivalent to 192 litres.

TOP 5 CONSUMERS OF OIL (USAGE PER DAY)	
USA	19,650,000 barrels
Canada	2,200,000 barrels
Puerto Rico	190,000 barrels
Cuba	163,000 barrels
Jamaica	66,000 barrels

FAST FACTS

- The centre of Greenland has sunk to 305 m below sea level due to the weight of the huge ice sheet that covers most of the island.

- At 86 m below sea level, Death Valley in California is the lowest place in the USA. It is also the hottest and driest with summer temperatures often exceeding 49°C.

- The USA is the world's third largest producer of oil — 7,800,000 barrels each day.

- The saguaro cactus only grows in the Sonoran desert in the USA. Saguaros can grow to 15 m tall and live for 175 years.

- Cuba is the fifth largest island in the region at 110,860 sq km.

POLITICAL MAP OF NORTH AMERICA

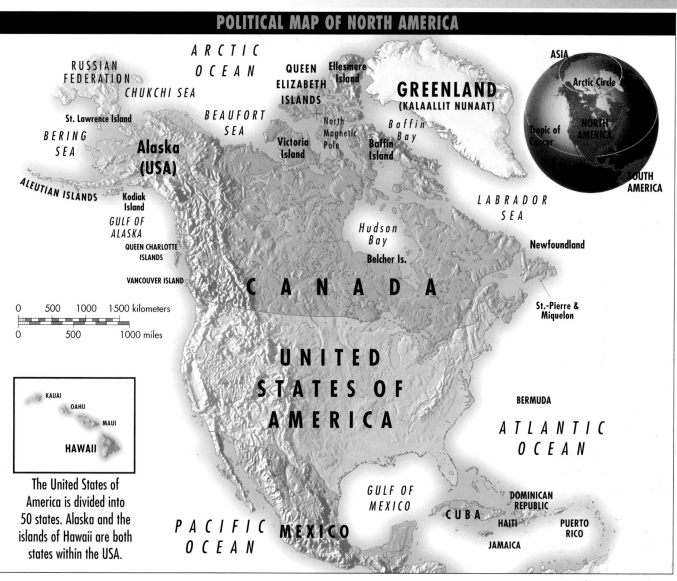

ARCTIC OCEAN

RUSSIAN FEDERATION

CHUKCHI SEA

QUEEN ELIZABETH ISLANDS

Ellesmere Island

GREENLAND
(KALAALLIT NUNAAT)

ASIA

Arctic Circle

NORTH AMERICA

Tropic of Cancer

SOUTH AMERICA

St. Lawrence Island

BERING SEA

Alaska (USA)

BEAUFORT SEA

Victoria Island

North Magnetic Pole

Baffin Island

Baffin Bay

ALEUTIAN ISLANDS

Kodiak Island

GULF OF ALASKA

QUEEN CHARLOTTE ISLANDS

VANCOUVER ISLAND

LABRADOR SEA

Hudson Bay

Belcher Is.

Newfoundland

CANADA

St.-Pierre & Miquelon

0	500	1000	1500 kilometers

0	500	1000 miles

UNITED STATES OF AMERICA

BERMUDA

ATLANTIC OCEAN

KAUAI
OAHU
MAUI
HAWAII

The United States of America is divided into 50 states. Alaska and the islands of Hawaii are both states within the USA.

PACIFIC OCEAN

MEXICO

GULF OF MEXICO

CUBA

DOMINICAN REPUBLIC

HAITI

PUERTO RICO

JAMAICA

POLITICAL MAP OF CENTRAL AMERICA AND THE CARIBBEAN

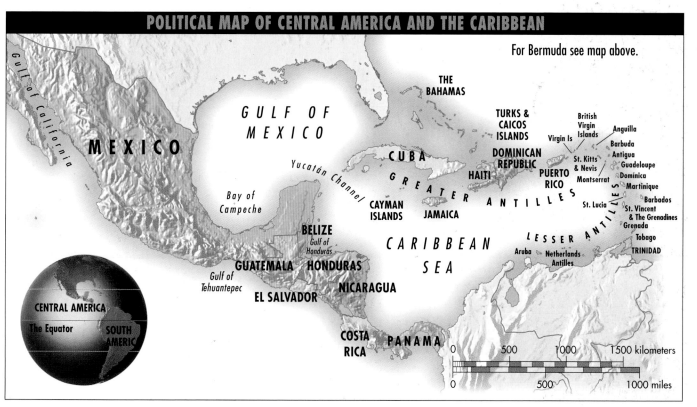

For Bermuda see map above.

Gulf of California

MEXICO

GULF OF MEXICO

THE BAHAMAS

TURKS & CAICOS ISLANDS

British Virgin Islands

Anguilla

Virgin Is

Barbuda

Antigua

Yucatán Channel

CUBA

DOMINICAN REPUBLIC

St. Kitts & Nevis

Guadeloupe

Bay of Campeche

HAITI

PUERTO RICO

Montserrat

Dominica

Martinique

GREATER ANTILLES

Barbados

CAYMAN ISLANDS

JAMAICA

St. Lucia

St. Vincent & The Grenadines

BELIZE

Gulf of Honduras

CARIBBEAN SEA

LESSER ANTILLES

Grenada

Tobago

GUATEMALA

HONDURAS

Aruba

Netherlands Antilles

TRINIDAD

Gulf of Tehuantepec

EL SALVADOR

NICARAGUA

CENTRAL AMERICA

The Equator

SOUTH AMERICA

COSTA RICA

PANAMA

0	500	1000	1500 kilometers

0	500	1000 miles

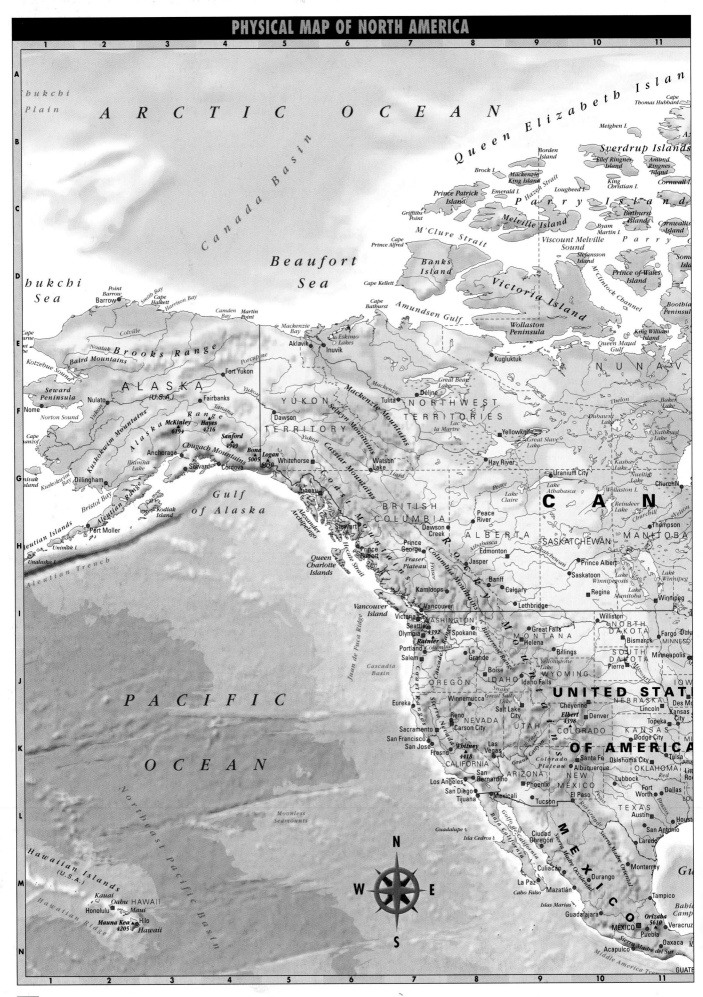

Miller Cylindrical Projection

	Land heights metres	Sea depths metres
■ Capital city		
■ Administrative capital	8000	500
	7000	1000
● Other city or town	6000	2000
▲ Mountain summit (heights in metres)	5000	4000
	4000	5000
⛭ Dry salt lake	3000	6000
⤳ Marsh	2000	7000
—— International boundary	1000	
	500	
……… International boundary, disputed	200	
–––– Administrative boundary	0	
	Land below sea level	

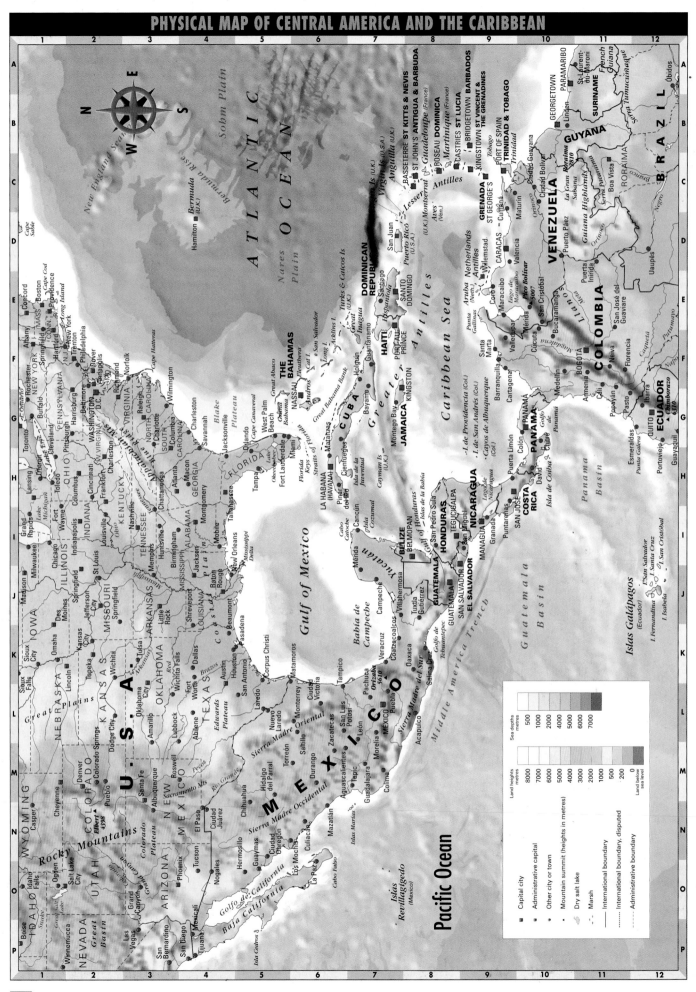

CLIMATE: NORTH AND CENTRAL AMERICA

TEMPERATURES IN JANUARY   **TEMPERATURES IN JULY**

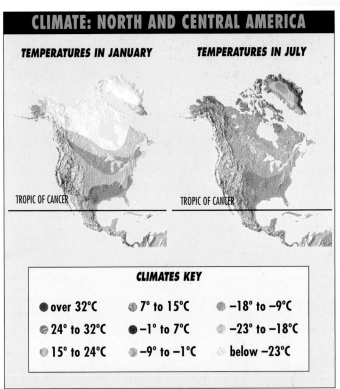

TROPIC OF CANCER   TROPIC OF CANCER

CLIMATES KEY

- ● over 32°C
- ◐ 7° to 15°C
- ◑ –18° to –9°C
- ◐ 24° to 32°C
- ● –1° to 7°C
- ◐ –23° to –18°C
- ◐ 15° to 24°C
- ◐ –9° to –1°C
- ◐ below –23°C

HABITATS: NORTH AND CENTRAL AMERICA

This map shows the different types of habitat across the continent.

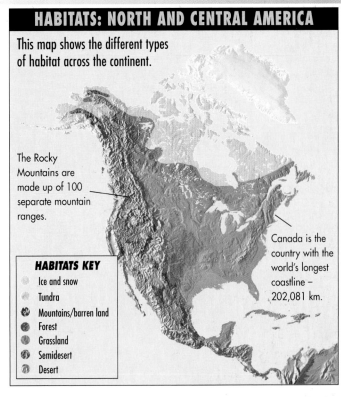

The Rocky Mountains are made up of 100 separate mountain ranges.

Canada is the country with the world's longest coastline – 202,081 km.

HABITATS KEY

- Ice and snow
- Tundra
- Mountains/barren land
- Forest
- Grassland
- Semidesert
- Desert

LAND USE: NORTH AND CENTRAL AMERICA

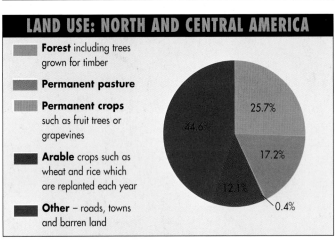

- **Forest** including trees grown for timber
- **Permanent pasture**
- **Permanent crops** such as fruit trees or grapevines
- **Arable** crops such as wheat and rice which are replanted each year
- **Other** – roads, towns and barren land

25.7%
44.6%
17.2%
12.1%
0.4%

SAN ANDREAS FAULT

The San Andreas fault on the Pacific coast of California, USA, is 1,200 km long.
The fault is part of the boundary between the Pacific and North American tectonic plates, and is one of the world's major earthquake zones.

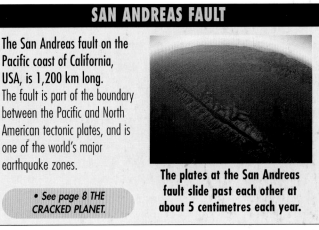

• See page 8 THE CRACKED PLANET.

The plates at the San Andreas fault slide past each other at about 5 centimetres each year.

NORTH AMERICA FACTFILES

Each country by country factfile contains: **total area** of the country in square kilometres; **total population;** name of the **capital city**; the main **currency** used in the country; **main languages spoken** (listed in order of number of speakers); **top five farming products produced** (listed in order of importance to the country's economy); **natural resources** (of commercial importance); and a country's **status** if it is not independent.

CANADA
Total area (sq km): 9,984,670
Total population: 32,805,041
Capital city: Ottawa
Currency: Canadian dollar (CAD)
Languages: English; French
Farming (top 5 products): Wheat; barley; oilseed; tobacco; fruit
Natural resources (top 5): Iron ore; nickel; zinc; copper; gold

GREENLAND
Total area (sq km): 2,166,086
Total population: 56,375
Capital city: Nuuk
Currency: Danish krone (DKK)
Languages: Greenlandic (Inuit mixed with Danish); Danish; English
Farming: Forage crops (for animals); vegetables; sheep; reindeer
Natural resources (top 5): Coal; iron ore; lead; zinc; molybdenum
Status: Self-governing Danish territory

SAINT PIERRE & MIQUELON
Total area (sq km): 242
Total population: 7012
Capital city: Saint-Pierre
Currency: Euro (EUR)
Languages: Creole
Farming: Vegetables; poultry; livestock
Natural resources: Fish
Status: French overseas territory

UNITED STATES OF AMERICA
Total area (sq km): 9,631,418
Total population: 295,734,134
Capital city: Washington DC
Currency: US dollar (USD)
Languages: English; Spanish
Farming (top 5 products): Wheat; corn and other cereal crops; fruit; vegetables; cotton
Natural resources (top 5): Coal; copper; lead; molybdenum; phosphates

• See the GLOSSARY for words and terms used in these FACTFILES.

• See page 22 CENTRAL AMERICA FACTFILES.

CENTRAL AMERICA
FACTFILES

Each country by country factfile contains: **total area** of the country in square kilometres; **total population**; name of the **capital city**; the main **currency** used in the country; **main languages spoken** (listed in order of number of speakers); **top five farming products produced** (listed in order of importance to the country's economy); **natural resources** (of commercial importance; some countries do not have natural resources, such as oil or minerals, but their coastline and climate attract tourists which are vital to the country's economy); and a country's **status** if it is not independent.

An inviting Virgin Islands' beach. For many countries the beauty of the environment is their most important natural resource.

• See the GLOSSARY for words and terms used in these FACTFILES.

ANGUILLA

Total area (sq km): 102
Total population: 13,254
Capital city: The Valley
Currency: East Caribbean dollar (XCD)
Languages: English
Farming: Tobacco; vegetables; cattle
Natural resources: Salt; fish; lobsters
Status: United Kingdom overseas territory

ANTIGUA AND BARBUDA
Total area (sq km): 442.6
Total population: 68,722
Capital city: Saint John's (on Antigua)
Currency: East Caribbean dollar (XCD)
Languages: English; local dialects
Farming (top 5 products): Cotton; vegetables; bananas; coconuts; cucumbers
Natural resources: Limited, but climate good for tourism

ARUBA
Total area (sq km): 193
Total population: 71,566
Capital city: Oranjestad
Currency: Aruban guilder/florin (AWG)
Languages: Dutch; Papiamento; English
Farming: Aloe plants; livestock
Natural resources: Fish; white sandy beaches which are good for tourism
Status: Self-governing Netherlands territory

BAHAMAS (THE)
Total area (sq km): 13,940
Total population: 301,790
Capital city: Nassau
Currency: Bahamian dollar (BSD)
Languages: English; Creole
Farming: Citrus fruits; vegetables; poultry
Natural resources: Salt; aragonite; timber

BARBADOS
Total area (sq km): 431
Total population: 279,254
Capital city: Bridgetown
Currency: Barbadian dollar (BCD)
Languages: English
Farming: Sugar cane; vegetables; cotton
Natural resources: Oil; fish; natural gas

BELIZE
Total area (sq km): 22,966
Total population: 279,457
Capital city: Belmopan
Currency: Belizean dollar (BZD)
Languages: English; Spanish; Mayan
Farming (top 5 products): Bananas; coca; citrus fruits; sugar cane; fish
Natural resources: Timber; fish; hydroelectric power

BERMUDA
Total area (sq km): 53.3
Total population: 63,365
Capital city: Hamilton
Currency: Bermudian dollar (BCD)
Languages: English; Portuguese
Farming (top 5 products): Bananas; vegetables; citrus fruits; cut flowers; dairy products
Natural resources: Limestone; climate good for tourism
Status: United Kingdom overseas territory

BRITISH VIRGIN ISLANDS
Total area (sq km): 153
Total population: 22,643
Capital city: Road Town
Currency: US dollar (USD)
Languages: English
Farming: Fruit; vegetables; livestock; poultry
Natural resources: Fish; islands good for tourism
Status: United Kingdom overseas territory

CAYMAN ISLANDS
Total area (sq km): 262
Total population: 44,270
Capital city: George Town
Currency: Caymanian dollar (KYD)
Languages: English
Farming: Vegetables; fruit; livestock; turtle farming
Natural resources: Fish; climate and beaches good for tourism
Status: United Kingdom overseas territory

COSTA RICA
Total area (sq km): 51,100
Total population: 4,016,173
Capital city: San Jose
Currency: Costa Rican colon (CRC)
Languages: Spanish; English
Farming (top 5 products): Coffee; pineapples; bananas; sugar cane; corn
Natural resources: Hydroelectric power

CUBA
Total area (sq km): 110,860
Total population: 11,346,670
Capital city: Havana
Currency: Cuban peso (CUP)
Languages: Spanish
Farming (top 5 products): Sugar cane; tobacco; citrus fruits; coffee; rice
Natural resources (top 5): Cobalt; nickel; iron ore; chromium; copper

DOMINICA
Total area (sq km): 754
Total population: 69,029
Capital city: Roseau
Currency: East Caribbean dollar (XCD)
Languages: English; French patois
Farming (top 5 products): Bananas; citrus fruits; mangos; root vegetables; coconuts
Natural resources: Timber; hydroelectric power

DOMINICAN REPUBLIC

Total area (sq km): 48,730
Total population: 8,950,034
Capital city: Santo Domingo
Currency: Dominican peso (DOP)
Languages: Spanish
Farming (top 5 products): Sugar cane; coffee; cotton; cocoa; tobacco
Natural resources: Nickel; bauxite; gold; silver

EL SALVADOR
Total area (sq km): 21,040
Total population: 6,704,932
Capital city: San Salvador
Currency: US dollar (USD)
Languages: Spanish; Nahua
Farming (top 5 products): Coffee; sugar cane; corn; rice; oilseed
Natural resources: Hydroelectric power; geothermal power; oil

GRENADA

Total area (sq km): 344
Total population: 89,502
Capital city: Saint George's
Currency: East Caribbean dollar (XCD)
Languages: English; French patois
Farming (top 5 products): Bananas; cocoa; nutmeg; mace; citrus fruits
Natural resources: Timber; tropical fruit; deepwater harbours (good for shipping)

GUADELOUPE

Total area (sq km): 1,780
Total population: 448,713
Capital city: Basse—Terre
Currency: Euro (EUR)
Languages: French
Farming (top 5 products): Bananas; sugar cane; fruit; vegetables; livestock
Natural resources: Limited, but beaches and climate good for tourism
Status: French overseas territory

GUATEMALA

Total area (sq km): 108,890
Total population: 14,655,189
Capital city: Guatemala
Currency: Quetzal (GTQ); US dollar (USD)
Languages: Spanish; Quiche; Cakchiquel; Kekchi; Mam
Farming (top 5 products): Sugar cane; corn; bananas; coffee; beans
Natural resources (top 5): Oil; nickel; timber; fish; chicle

HAITI

Total area (sq km): 27,750
Total population: 8,121,622
Capital city: Port—au—Prince
Currency: Gourde (HTG)
Languages: French; Creole
Farming (top 5 products): Coffee; mangos; sugar cane; rice; corn
Natural resources (top 5): Bauxite; copper; calcium carbonate; gold; marble

HONDURAS

Total area (sq km): 112,090
Total population: 6,975,204
Capital city: Tegucigalpa
Currency: Lempira (HNL)
Languages: Spanish; Amerindian dialects
Farming (top 5 products): Bananas; coffee; citrus fruits; cattle; timber
Natural resources (top 5): Timber; gold; silver; copper; lead

JAMAICA

Total area (sq km): 10,991
Total population: 2,731,832
Capital city: Kingston
Currency: Jamaican dollar (JMD)
Languages: English; English patois
Farming (top 5 products): Sugar cane; bananas; coffee; citrus fruits; yams
Natural resources: Bauxite; gypsum; limestone

MARTINIQUE

Total area (sq km): 1,100
Total population: 432,900
Capital city: Fort-de-France
Currency: Euro (EUR)
Languages: French; Creole patois
Farming (top 5 products): Pineapples; avocados; bananas; cut flowers; vegetables
Natural resources: Limited, but coastline and beaches good for tourism
Status: French overseas territory

MEXICO

Total area (sq km): 1,972,550
Total population: 106,202,903
Capital city: Mexico City (Distrito Federal)
Currency: Mexican peso (MXN)
Languages: Spanish; Mayan; Nahuatl
Farming (top 5 products): Corn; wheat; soybeans; rice; beans
Natural resources (top 5): Oil; silver; copper; gold; lead

MONTSERRAT

Total area (sq km): 102
Total population: 9,341
Capital city: Temporary government buildings at Brades Estate, Carr's Bay and Little Bay due to 1997 volcano
Currency: East Caribbean dollar (XCD)
Languages: English
Farming (top 5 products): Cabbages; carrots; cucumbers; tomatoes; onions
Natural resources: Very limited
Status: United Kingdom overseas territory

NICARAGUA

Total area (sq km): 129,494
Total population: 5,465,100
Capital city: Managua
Currency: Gold cordoba (NIO)
Languages: Spanish
Farming (top 5 products): Coffee; bananas; sugar cane; cotton; rice
Natural resources (top 5): Gold; silver; copper; tungsten; lead

PANAMA

Total area (sq km): 78,200
Total population: 3,039,150
Capital city: Panama
Currency: Balboa (PAB); US dollar (USD)
Languages: Spanish; English
Farming (top 5 products): Bananas; rice; corn; coffee; sugar cane
Natural resources: Copper; timber; shrimps; hydroelectric power

PUERTO RICO

Total area (sq km): 9,104
Total population: 3,916,632
Capital city: San Juan
Currency: US dollar (USD)
Languages: Spanish; English
Farming (top 5 products): Sugar cane; coffee; pineapples; plantains; bananas
Natural resources: Copper and nickel (limited amounts); potential for onshore and offshore oil
Status: United States of America Commonwealth

ST KITTS AND NEVIS

Total area (sq km): 261
Total population: 38,958
Capital city: Basseterre
Currency: East Caribbean dollar (XCD)
Languages: English
Farming (top 5 products): Sugar cane; rice; yams; vegetables; bananas
Natural resources: Arable land

ST LUCIA

Total area (sq km): 616
Total population: 166,312
Capital city: Castries
Currency: East Caribbean dollar (XCD)
Languages: English; French patois
Farming (top 5 products): Bananas; coconuts; vegetables; citrus fruits; root vegetables
Natural resources (top 5): Forests; beaches (for tourism); pumice; mineral springs; potential for geothermal power

ST VINCENT AND THE GRENADINES

Total area (sq km): 389
Total population: 117,534
Capital city: Kingstown
Currency: East Caribbean dollar (XCD)
Languages: English; French patois
Farming (top 5 products): Bananas; coconuts; sweet potatoes; spices; livestock
Natural resources: Hydroelectric power

TRINIDAD AND TOBAGO

Total area (sq km): 5,128
Total population: 1,088,644
Capital city: Port—of—Spain
Currency: Trinidad and Tobago dollar (TTD)
Languages: English; Hindi; French; Spanish; Chinese
Farming (top 5 products): Cocoa; sugar cane; rice; citrus fruits; coffee
Natural resources: Oil; natural gas; asphalt

TURKS AND CAICOS ISLANDS

Total area (sq km): 430
Total population: 20,556
Capital city: Grand Turk
Currency: US dollar (USD)
Languages: English
Farming: Corn; beans; cassava; citrus fruits
Natural resources: Fish; spiny lobsters; conch (tropical marine molluscs)
Status: United Kingdom overseas territory

VIRGIN ISLANDS

Total area (sq km): 352
Total population: 108,708
Capital city: Charlotte Amalie
Currency: US dollar (USD)
Languages: English; Spanish or Spanish Creole; French or French Creole
Farming: Fruit; vegetables; sorghum; cattle
Natural resources: Limited, but climate and beaches good for tourism
Status: United States of America unincorporated territory

Opened in 1914, the 80-kilometre-long, manmade Panama Canal allows ships to sail from the Pacific Ocean to the Atlantic Ocean. Before the canal was built, ships had to sail all the way around South America via Cape Horn.

SOUTH AMERICA

PEOPLE FACTFILE

Total population of continent:
371,400,000

Highest population:
Brazil 186,112,794

Lowest population:
Paraguay 6,347,884

Most populous city:
São Paulo, Brazil
18,333,000 residents

Average life expectancy:
Male: 70 years
Female: 76 years

Highest infant mortality rate:
Bolivia: 53 deaths per 1000 births

* See the GLOSSARY for definitions of LIFE EXPECTANCY and INFANT MORTALITY RATE.

Average annual income per person:
Highest: Uruguay £8,167
Lowest: Bolivia £1,464

GEOGRAPHY FACTFILE

Total land area:
17,793,000 sq km

Largest country:
Brazil: 8,511,965 sq km
Fifth largest country in the world

Smallest country:
Netherlands Antilles:
960 sq km

Largest island:
Isla Grande de Tierra del Fuego
47,000 sq km

Largest desert:
Atacama Desert, Chile
80,000 sq km
There has never been any rainfall recorded in parts of this desert.

Highest waterfall:
Angel Falls, Venezuela
Total drop: 979 m

• See page 27 SOUTH AMERICA FACTFILES.

The continent of South America stretches from the warm waters of the Caribbean Sea in the north to the stormy, cold waters of Cape Horn in the south. The world's longest mountain chain, the Andes, runs down the western coast, while the dense, dark Amazon forest, the world's largest rainforest, spreads across the north of the continent.

The Amazon River accounts for 20% of all the freshwater that drains into the world's oceans each year.

HIGHEST MOUNTAINS (BY COUNTRY)

NAME	LOCATION	HEIGHT (metres)
Aconcagua	Argentina	6,960*
Ojos del Salado	Argentina/Chile	6,980
Huascaran	Peru	6,768
Sajama	Bolivia	6,542
Chimborazo	Ecuador	6,310

* Aconcagua is the highest mountain in South America.

• See page 10 THE ANDES.

LONGEST RIVERS

NAME	RIVER MOUTH	LENGTH (km)
Amazon	Atlantic Ocean	6,450
Parana	Atlantic Ocean	4,500
Purus	Amazon	3,350
Madeira	Amazon	3,200

LARGEST LAKES

NAME		AREA (sq km)
Lake Titicaca	Bolivia/Peru	8,300
Lake Poopo	Bolivia	2,800

HABITATS: SOUTH AMERICA

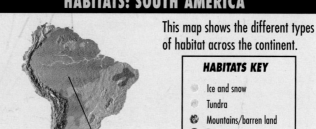

This map shows the different types of habitat across the continent.

The Amazon rainforest

HABITATS KEY
- Ice and snow
- Tundra
- Mountains/barren land
- Forest
- Grassland
- Semidesert
- Desert

AMAZON RAINFOREST FACTS

Rainforests around the world are shrinking. They are cut down by the timber industry or cleared for mineral mining and farming.

- Just 2.5 acres of Amazon rainforest can contain up to 1500 different plant species. Each species of tree may support more than 400 different insect species.

- 20% of the world's birds live in the Amazon rainforest.

- 500 years ago, 6 million native people lived in the Amazon rainforest. In 2000, the number was less than 250,000.

FAST FACTS

- Venezuela is South America's main producer of oil. Brazil uses the most oil in South America, 2,199,000 barrels each day.

- The Amazon river's source is a remote slope of the Nevado Mismi peak (5,316 m high), in Peru.

- At around 3,650 m above sea level, La Paz in Bolivia is the world's highest capital city.

POLITICAL MAP OF SOUTH AMERICA

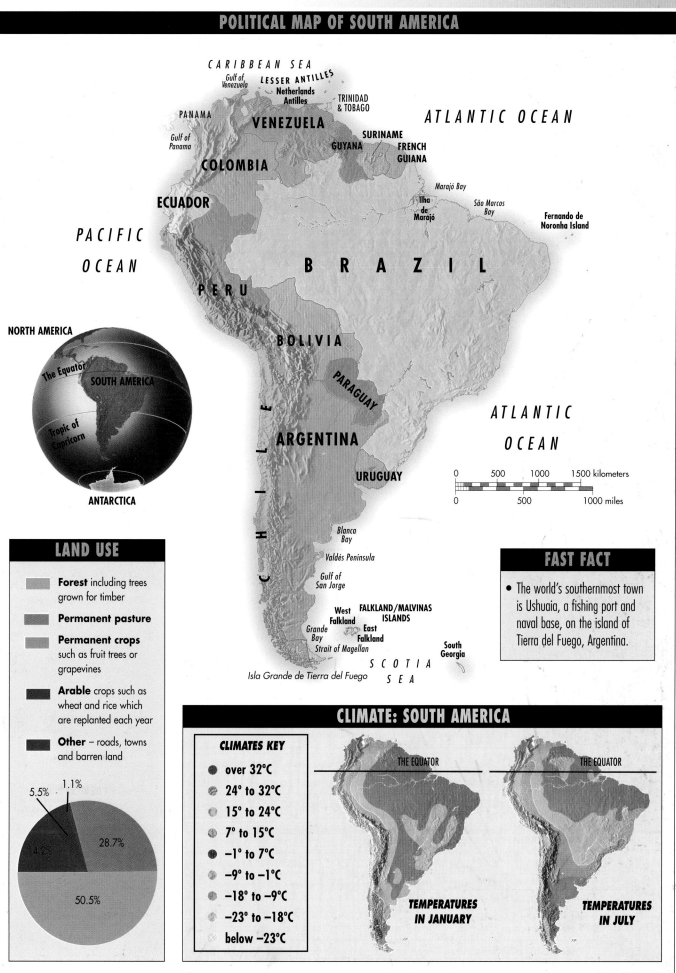

CARIBBEAN SEA

Gulf of Venezuela

LESSER ANTILLES

Netherlands Antilles

TRINIDAD & TOBAGO

PANAMA

ATLANTIC OCEAN

VENEZUELA

Gulf of Panama

SURINAME

GUYANA

FRENCH GUIANA

COLOMBIA

ECUADOR

Marajó Bay

Ilha de Marajó

São Marcos Bay

Fernando de Noronha Island

PACIFIC OCEAN

B R A Z I L

PERU

NORTH AMERICA

The Equator

SOUTH AMERICA

Tropic of Capricorn

ANTARCTICA

BOLIVIA

PARAGUAY

ATLANTIC OCEAN

ARGENTINA

URUGUAY

C H I L E

0   500   1000   1500 kilometers

0   500   1000 miles

Blanca Bay

Valdés Peninsula

Gulf of San Jorge

West Falkland

FALKLAND/MALVINAS ISLANDS

Grande Bay

East Falkland

South Georgia

Strait of Magellan

Isla Grande de Tierra del Fuego

S C O T I A S E A

LAND USE

- **Forest** including trees grown for timber
- **Permanent pasture**
- **Permanent crops** such as fruit trees or grapevines
- **Arable** crops such as wheat and rice which are replanted each year
- **Other** – roads, towns and barren land

5.5%
1.1%
28.7%
14.2%
50.5%

FAST FACT

- The world's southernmost town is Ushuaia, a fishing port and naval base, on the island of Tierra del Fuego, Argentina.

CLIMATE: SOUTH AMERICA

CLIMATES KEY

- over 32°C
- 24° to 32°C
- 15° to 24°C
- 7° to 15°C
- –1° to 7°C
- –9° to –1°C
- –18° to –9°C
- –23° to –18°C
- below –23°C

THE EQUATOR

THE EQUATOR

TEMPERATURES IN JANUARY

TEMPERATURES IN JULY

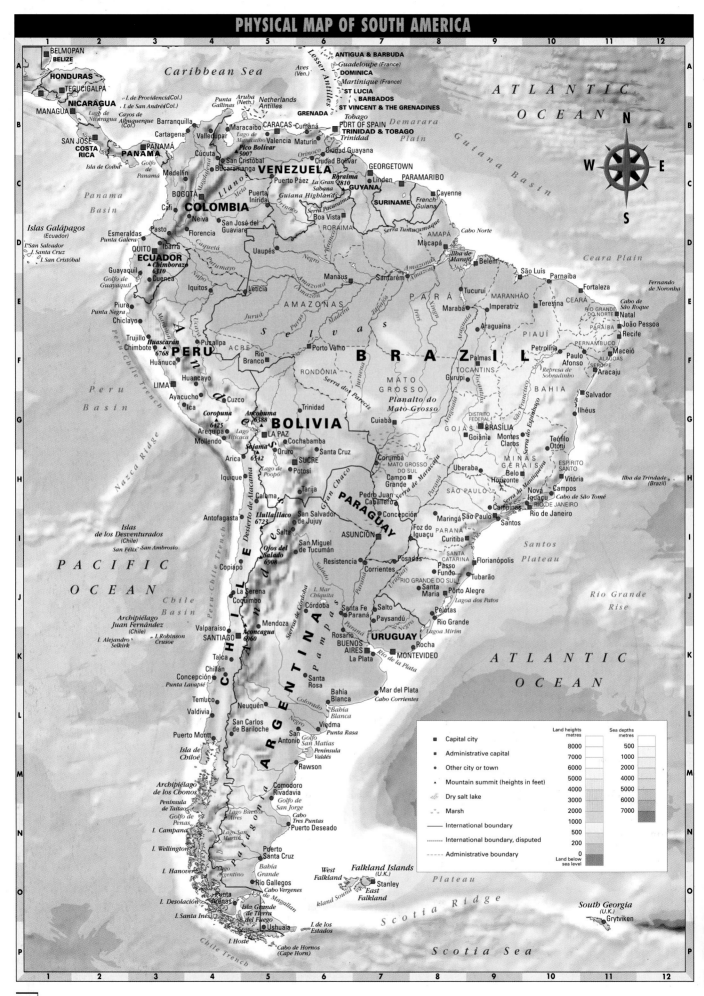

SOUTH AMERICA FACTFILES

Each country by country factfile contains: **total area** of the country in square kilometres; **total population**; name of the **capital city**; the main **currency** used in the country; **main languages spoken** (listed in order of number of speakers); **top five farming products produced** (listed in order of importance to the country's economy); **natural resources** (of commercial importance); and a country's **status** if it is not independent.

ARGENTINA
Total area (sq km): 2,766,890
Total population: 39,537,943
Capital city: Buenos Aires
Currency: Argentine peso (ARS)
Languages: Spanish; English; Italian; German; French
Farming (top 5 products): Sunflower seeds; lemons; soybeans; grapes; corn
Natural resources (top 5): Fertile pampas plains; lead; zinc; tin; copper

BOLIVIA
Total area (sq km): 1,098,580
Total population: 8,857,870
Capital city: La Paz/Sucre
Currency: Boliviano (BOB)
Languages: Spanish; Quechua; Aymara
Farming (top 5 products): Soybeans; coffee; coca; cotton; corn
Natural resources (top 5): Tin; natural gas; oil; zinc; tungsten

BRAZIL
Total area (sq km): 8,511,965
Total population: 186,112,794
Capital city: Brasilia
Currency: Real (BRL)
Languages: Portuguese; Spanish; English; French
Farming (top 5 products): Coffee; soybeans; wheat; rice; corn
Natural resources (top 5): Bauxite; gold; iron ore; manganese; nickel

CHILE
Total area (sq km): 756,950
Total population: 15,980,912
Capital city: Santiago
Currency: Chilean peso (CLP)
Languages: Spanish
Farming (top 5 products): Fruit; onions; wheat; corn; oats
Natural resources (top 5): Copper; timber; iron ore; nitrates; precious metals

COLOMBIA
Total area (sq km): 1,138,910
Total population: 42,954,279
Capital city: Bogota
Currency: Colombian peso (COP)
Languages: Spanish
Farming (top 5 products): Coffee; cut flowers; bananas; rice; tobacco
Natural resources (top 5): Oil; natural gas; coal; iron ore; nickel

ECUADOR
Total area (sq km): 283,560
Total population: 13,363,593
Capital city: Quito
Currency: US dollar (USD)
Languages: Spanish; Quechua
Farming (top 5 products): Bananas; coffee; cocoa; rice; potatoes
Natural resources: Oil; fish; timber; hydroelectric power

FRENCH GUIANA
Total area (sq km): 91,000
Total population: 195,506
Capital city: Cayenne
Currency: Euro (EUR)
Languages: French
Farming (top 5 products): Corn; rice; manioc (cassava); sugar cane; cocoa
Natural resources (top 5): Bauxite; timber; gold; oil; kaolin
Status: French overseas territory

GUYANA
Total area (sq km): 214,970
Total population: 765,283
Capital city: Georgetown
Currency: Guyanese dollar (GYD)
Languages: English; Amerindian dialects; Creole; Hindi
Farming (top 5 products): Sugar cane; rice; wheat; vegetable oils; livestock
Natural resources (top 5): Bauxite; gold; diamonds; timber; shrimp

NETHERLANDS ANTILLES
Total area (sq km): 960
Total population: 219,958
Capital city: Willestad
Currency: Netherlands Antillean guilder (ANG)
Languages: Papiamento; English; Dutch
Farming (top 5 products): Aloe plants; sorghum; peanuts; vegetables; tropical fruit
Natural resources: Phosphates (on Curacao island); salt (on Bonaire island)
Status: Self-governing Netherlands territory

PARAGUAY
Total area (sq km): 406,750
Total population: 6,347,884
Capital city: Asuncion
Currency: Guarani (PYG)
Languages: Spanish; Guarani
Farming (top 5 products): Cotton; sugar cane; soybeans; corn; wheat
Natural resources (top 5): Hydroelectric power; timber; iron ore; manganese; limestone

PERU
Total area (sq km): 1,285,220
Total population: 27,925,628
Capital city: Lima
Currency: Nuevo sol (PEN)
Languages: Spanish; Quechua; Aymara
Farming (top 5 products): Coffee; cotton; sugar cane; rice; potatoes
Natural resources (top 5): Copper; silver; gold; oil; timber

SURINAME
Total area (sq km): 163,270
Total population: 438,144
Capital city: Paramaribo
Currency: Suriname guilder (SRG)
Languages: Dutch; English; Sranang Tongo (Creole language sometimes called Taki–Taki)
Farming (top 5 products): Rice; bananas; palm kernels; coconuts; plantains
Natural resources (top 5): Timber; hydroelectric power; fish; kaolin; shrimp

URUGUAY
Total area (sq km): 176,220
Total population: 3,415,920
Capital city: Montevideo
Currency: Uruguayan peso (UYU)
Languages: Spanish
Farming (top 5 products): Rice; wheat; corn; barley; livestock
Natural resources: Hydroelectric power; minerals; fish

VENEZUELA
Total area (sq km): 912,050
Total population: 25,375,281
Capital city: Caracas
Currency: Bolivar (VEB)
Languages: Spanish; numerous indigenous dialects
Farming (top 5 products): Corn; sorghum; sugar cane; rice; bananas
Natural resources (top 5): Oil; natural gas; iron ore; gold; bauxite

• See the GLOSSARY for words and terms used in these FACTFILES.

Llamas are members of the camel family and are native to South America. They have lived in the Andes for centuries, both as wild animals and in domesticated herds. Today, they still work as pack animals carrying goods through inaccessible mountain passes.

AFRICA

GEOGRAPHY FACTFILE

Total land area:
30,302,000 sq km

Largest country:
Sudan: 2,505,810 sq km

Smallest country:
Mayotte: 374 sq km

Largest lake:
Lake Victoria, East Africa
69,000 sq km

Largest desert:
Sahara Desert, North Africa
9,000,000 sq km
Largest desert in the world

Highest waterfall:
Tugela Falls, South Africa
Total drop: 948 m (in five steps)

• See page 33 AFRICA FACTFILES.

Africa is the second largest continent in the world. The world's biggest desert, the Sahara dominates the landscape of the north, while in the south forests and vast grasslands are home to wild animals, such as leopards, lions and elephants. The *Great Rift Valley*, one of the Earth's major geological features, runs from the Red Sea down to Mozambique. This huge crack in the Earth's surface (caused by a series of faults) is made up of mountains, volcanoes, deep valleys and lakes.

An African leopard in the Samburu Game Reserve, Kenya.

HIGHEST MOUNTAINS

NAME	LOCATION	HEIGHT (metres)
Mt Kilimanjaro	Tanzania	5,895
Mt Kirinyaga (Mt Kenya)	Kenya	5,200
Mount Stanley (Margherita Peak)	Dem. Rep. Congo/Uganda	5,110
Ras Dashen	Ethiopia	4,620

LONGEST RIVERS

NAME	RIVER MOUTH	LENGTH (km)
Nile	Mediterranean	6,670
Congo	Atlantic Ocean	4,467
Niger	Atlantic Ocean	4,180
Zambezi	Indian Ocean	3,540

LARGEST ISLANDS

NAME		AREA (sq km)
Madagascar	Indian Ocean	587,040
Réunion	Indian Ocean	2,517

• See page 11 WORLD'S 10 LARGEST LAKES.

OIL CONSUMPTION

The amount of oil produced, bought and sold, and used in the world is measured in barrels. A barrel is equivalent to 192 litres.

Nigeria is Africa's largest producer of oil – 2,356,000 barrels per day

TOP 5 CONSUMERS OF OIL (USAGE PER DAY)	
Egypt	562,000 barrels
South Africa	460,000 barrels
Nigeria	275,000 barrels
Libya	216,000 barrels
Algeria	209,000 barrels

FAST FACTS

• Almost 90% of the rainforest in West Africa has been destroyed.

• 90% of the rainforest on the African island of Madagascar has been destroyed. Around 80% of the animal species found on Madagascar live only on this island and nowhere else on Earth (excluding zoo populations).

• See page 24 AMAZON RAINFOREST FACTS.

• Namibia was the first country in the world to include protecting the environment in its constitution. Around 14% of Namibia is now protected including the entire Namib Desert coast.

• Ancient rock paintings show that 8000 years ago the Sahara Desert was a lush, green place that was home to many wild animals.

• It is believed that the first place in the world to cultivate coffee was Ethiopia. It was grown in the Kefa region of Ethiopia around 1000 years ago.

POLITICAL MAP OF AFRICA

0   500   1000   1500 kilometers
0   500   1000 miles

Madeira

Canary Is.

MOROCCO

TUNISIA

MEDITERRANEANE SEA

ALGERIA

LIBYA

EGYPT

WESTERN SAHARA

RED SEA

Cape Verde Is.

MAURITANIA

MALI

NIGER

CHAD

SUDAN

ERITREA

SENEGAL

GAMBIA

GUINEA BISSAU

GUINEA

BURKINO FASO

BENIN

GHANA

NIGERIA

DJIBOUTI

SIERRA LEONE

COTE D'IVOIRE

CENTRAL AFRICAN REPUBLIC

ETHIOPIA

SOMALIA

LIBERIA

TOGO

CAMEROON

ATLANTIC OCEAN

EQUATORIAL GUINEA

SÃO TOMÉ & PRINCIPE

REPUBLIC OF CONGO

GABON

DEMOCRATIC REPUBLIC OF CONGO

UGANDA

KENYA

INDIAN OCEAN

RWANDA

BURUNDI

SEYCHELLES

TANZANIA

ANGOLA

ZAMBIA

MALAWI

COMOROS

Mayotte

NAMIBIA

ZIMBABWE

MOZAMBIQUE

MADAGASCAR

Mauritius

Réunion

BOTSWANA

SWAZILAND

SOUTH AFRICA

LESOTHO

(globe inset) EUROPE — Tropic of Cancer — AFRICA — The Equator — Tropic of Capricorn

MOUNT KILIMANJARO

Africa's Mount Kilimanjaro is an extinct volcano. It is the highest mountain in the world that it is possible to climb without specialist climbing skills or equipment. Around 22,000 people climb Kilimanjaro every year, making it the world's most climbed mountain.

Due to rainforest destruction many Madagascan animals, such as this ring-tailed lemur, are endangered.

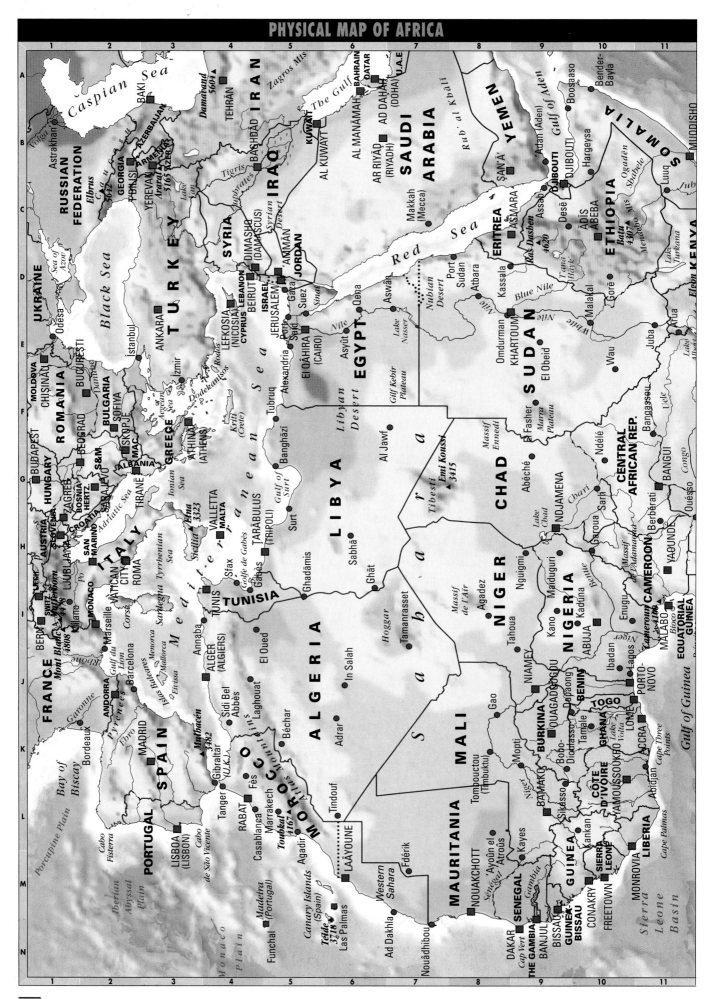

PHYSICAL MAP OF AFRICA

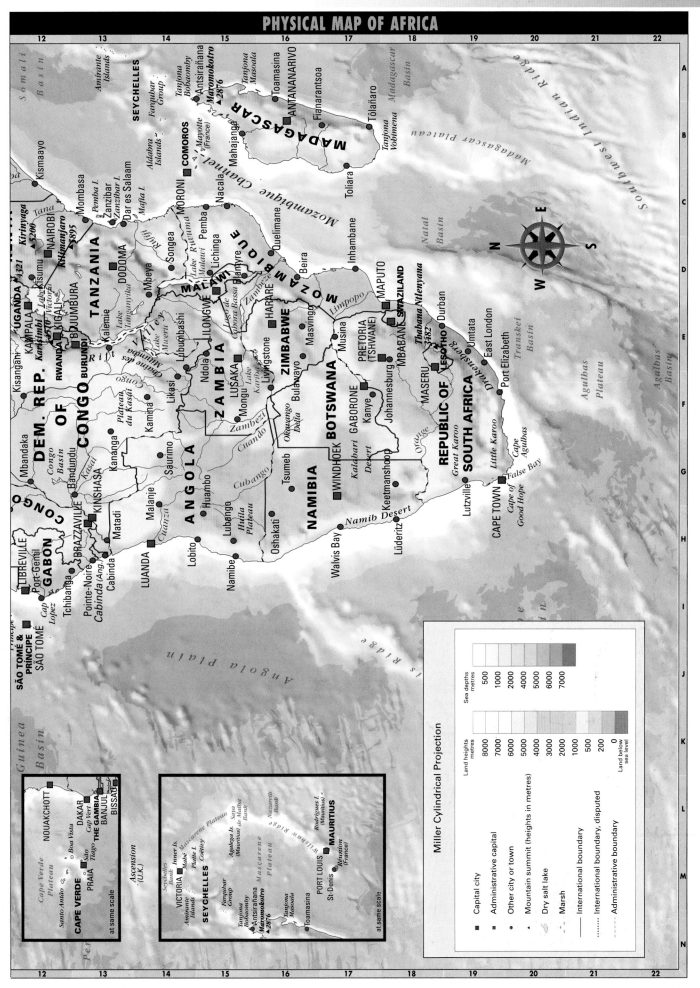

Somali Basin

SEYCHELLES
Amirante Islands
Farquhar Group
Aldabra Islands

Kismaayo
Mombasa
Pemba I.
Zanzibar
Zanzibar I.
Mafia I.
Dar es Salaam

COMOROS
MORONI
Mayotte (France)
Mozambique Channel

Tanjona Bobaomby
Antsirañana
Maromokotro ▲2876
Tanjona Masoala
Toamasina
ANTANANARIVO
MADAGASCAR
Fianarantsoa
Tanjona Vohimena
Tolañaro

Madagascar Plateau

Southwest Indian Ridge

Kirinyaga ▲5200
NAIROBI
Kilimanjaro ▲5895
Kisumu
Lake Victoria

UGANDA ▲4321
KAMPALA
Kisangani
Karisimbi
RWANDA
KIGALI
BUJUMBURA
BURUNDI

Tana

TANZANIA
DODOMA
Songea
Mbeya
Lake Tanganyika
Kalemie
Lake Rukwa
Ruvuma
Pemba
Lichinga
Lake Malawi

Nacala
Quelimane
Beira
Inhambane

Natal Basin

DEM. REP. OF CONGO
Kisangani
Congo
Lake Mweru
Plateau du Kasai
Kamina
Kananga
Kasai
Likasi
Lubumbashi

Great Rift Valley

MALAWI
LILONGWE
Lago de Cabora Bassa
Blantyre
Zambezi
HARARE
ZIMBABWE
Masvingo
Bulawayo
Livingstone
Lake Kariba

ZAMBIA
LUSAKA
Ndola
Mongu
Zambezi
Cuando

MOZAMBIQUE
Limpopo
MAPUTO
SWAZILAND
MBABANE
Thabana Ntlenyana ▲3482
MASERU
LESOTHO
Musina
PRETORIA (TSHWANE)
Johannesburg
Durban
Umtata
East London
Port Elizabeth

Drakensberg
Transkei Basin
Agulhas Plateau
Agulhas Basin

ANGOLA
Saurimo
Cuanza
Malanje
Huambo
Lubango
Huila Plateau
Oshakati
Cubango
Okavango Delta
Cuito

BOTSWANA
GABORONE
Kanye
Kalahari Desert
WINDHOEK
NAMIBIA
Tsumeb
Keetmanshoop
Orange
Great Karoo
Little Karoo
REPUBLIC OF SOUTH AFRICA
Lutzville
CAPE TOWN
Cape of Good Hope
False Bay
Cape Agulhas

Namib Desert
Walvis Bay
Lüderitz
Namibe

Kananga
Mbandaka
Congo Basin
Bandundu
BRAZZAVILLE
KINSHASA
Matadi
CONGO
GABON
LIBREVILLE
Port-Gentil
Cap Lopez
Tchibanga
Pointe-Noire
Cabinda (Ang.)
Cabinda
LUANDA

SÃO TOMÉ & PRÍNCIPE
SÃO TOMÉ
Príncipe

Lobito

Guinea Basin

Angola Plain

Walvis Ridge

Inset (bottom left)
NOUAKCHOTT
Cape Verde Plateau
DAKAR
THE GAMBIA
BANJUL
BISSAU
Cap Vert
Boa Vista
São Tiago
PRAIA
CAPE VERDE
Santo Antão
Ascension (U.K.)
Peru
at same scale

Inset (bottom centre)
Seychelles Bank
Inner Is.
Mahé
Platte I.
VICTORIA
SEYCHELLES
Amirante Islands
Farquhar Group
Tanjona Bobaomby
Antsirañana
Maromokotro ▲2876
Tanjona Masoala
Toamasina
Mascarene Plateau
Coëtivy
Agalega Is. (Mauritius)
Saya de Malha Bank
Nazareth Bank
Mascarene Plateau
Rodrigues I. (Mauritius)
MAURITIUS
Réunion (France)
PORT LOUIS
St-Denis
at same scale

Mid Indian Ridge

Legend
Miller Cylindrical Projection

Sea depths metres
500
1000
2000
4000
5000
6000
7000

Land heights metres
8000
7000
6000
5000
4000
3000
2000
1000
500
200
0 Land below sea level

■ Capital city
■ Administrative capital
● Other city or town
▲ Mountain summit (heights in metres)
Dry salt lake
Marsh
—— International boundary
········· International boundary, disputed
----- Administrative boundary

HABITATS: AFRICA

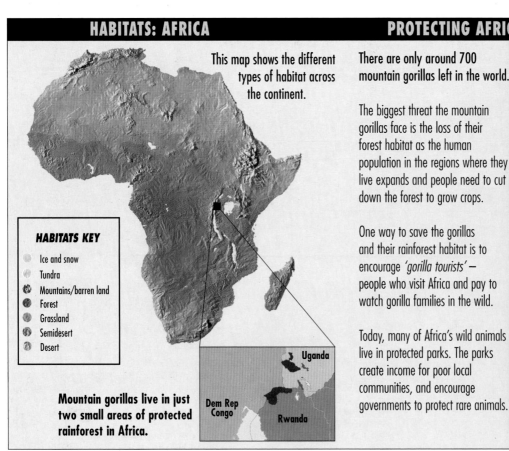

This map shows the different types of habitat across the continent.

HABITATS KEY

- Ice and snow
- Tundra
- Mountains/barren land
- Forest
- Grassland
- Semidesert
- Desert

Mountain gorillas live in just two small areas of protected rainforest in Africa.

Uganda

Dem Rep Congo

Rwanda

PROTECTING AFRICA'S WILDLIFE

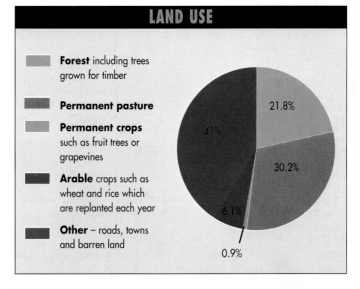

There are only around 700 mountain gorillas left in the world.

The biggest threat the mountain gorillas face is the loss of their forest habitat as the human population in the regions where they live expands and people need to cut down the forest to grow crops.

One way to save the gorillas and their rainforest habitat is to encourage *'gorilla tourists'* — people who visit Africa and pay to watch gorilla families in the wild.

Today, many of Africa's wild animals live in protected parks. The parks create income for poor local communities, and encourage governments to protect rare animals.

CLIMATE: AFRICA

TEMPERATURES IN JANUARY

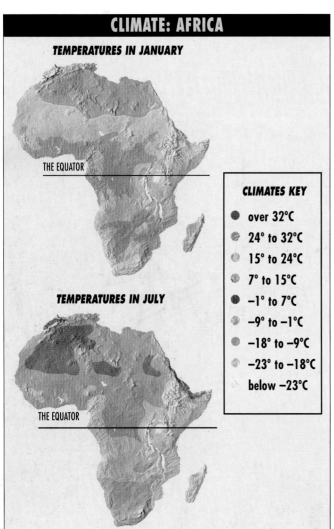

THE EQUATOR

TEMPERATURES IN JULY

THE EQUATOR

CLIMATES KEY

- over 32°C
- 24° to 32°C
- 15° to 24°C
- 7° to 15°C
- −1° to 7°C
- −9° to −1°C
- −18° to −9°C
- −23° to −18°C
- below −23°C

LAND USE

- **Forest** including trees grown for timber
- **Permanent pasture**
- **Permanent crops** such as fruit trees or grapevines
- **Arable** crops such as wheat and rice which are replanted each year
- **Other** – roads, towns and barren land

21.8%

41%

30.2%

6.1%

0.9%

THE AFRICAN BAOBAB TREE

The baobab tree grows in semi-arid places in Sub-Saharan Africa.

The tree can grow to 24 m tall with a diameter around the trunk of over 9 m. It is believed that baobabs can live for 1000 years.

Arabian legend says the devil plucked the baobab tree from the ground, then plunged it back in, upside-down!

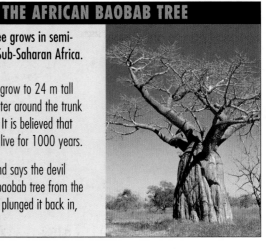

AFRICA FACTFILES

Each country by country factfile contains: **total area** of the country in square kilometres; **total population**; name of the **capital city**; the main **currency** used in the country; **main languages spoken** (listed in order of number of speakers); **top five farming products produced** (listed in order of importance to the country's economy); **natural resources** (of commercial importance); and a country's **status** if it is not independent.

ALGERIA
Total area (sq km): 2,381,740
Total population: 32,531,853
Capital city: Algiers
Currency: Algerian dinar (DZD)
Languages: Arabic; French; Berber dialects
Farming (top 5 products): Wheat; barley; oats; grapes; olives
Natural resources (top 5): Oil; natural gas; iron ore; phosphates; uranium

ANGOLA
Total area (sq km): 1,246,700
Total population: 11,190,786
Capital city: Luanda
Currency: Kwanza (AOA)
Languages: Portuguese; Bantu
Farming (top 5 products): Bananas; sugar cane; coffee; sisal; corn
Natural resources (top 5): Oil; diamonds; iron ore; phosphates; copper

BENIN
Total area (sq km): 112,620
Total population: 7,460,025
Capital city: Porto-Novo/Cotonou
Currency: Communaute Financiere Africaine franc (XOF)
Languages: French; Fon; Yoruba
Farming (top 5 products): Cotton; corn; cassava; yams; beans
Natural resources: Oil; limestone; marble; timber

BOTSWANA
Total area (sq km): 600,370
Total population: 1,640,115
Capital city: Gaborone
Currency: Pula (BWP)
Languages: Setswana; Kalanga
Farming (top 5 products): Livestock; sorghum; maize; millet; beans
Natural resources (top 5): Diamonds; copper; nickel; salt; coal

BURKINA FASO
Total area (sq km): 274,200
Total population: 13,925,313
Capital city: Ouagadougou
Currency: Communaute Financiere Africaine franc (XOF)
Languages: Moore; Jula; French
Farming (top 5 products): Cotton; peanuts; shea nuts; sesame; sorghum
Natural resources (top 5): Manganese; limestone; marble; gold; pumice

BURUNDI
Total area (sq km): 27,830
Total population: 6,370,609
Capital city: Bujumbura
Currency: Burundi franc (BIF)
Languages: Kirundi; French; Swahili
Farming (top 5 products): Coffee; cotton; tea; corn; sorghum
Natural resources (top 5): Nickel; uranium; peat; cobalt; copper

CAMEROON
Total area (sq km): 475,440
Total population: 16,380,005
Capital city: Yaounde
Currency: Communaute Financiere Africaine franc (XAF)
Languages: English; French; 24 African languages
Farming (top 5 products): Coffee; cocoa; cotton; rubber; bananas
Natural resources (top 5): Oil; bauxite; iron ore; timber; hydroelectric power

CAPE VERDE
Total area (sq km): 4,033
Total population: 418,224
Capital city: Praia
Currency: Cape Verdean escudo (CVE)
Languages: Portuguese; Crioulo
Farming (top 5 products): Bananas; corn; beans; sweet potatoes; sugar cane
Natural resources (top 5): Salt; basalt rock; limestone; kaolin; fish

CENTRAL AFRICAN REPUBLIC
Total area (sq km): 622,984
Total population: 3,799,897
Capital city: Bangui
Currency: Communaute Financiere Africaine franc (XAF)
Languages: French; Sangho
Farming (top 5 products): Cotton; coffee; tobacco; cassava; yams
Natural resources (top 5): Diamonds; uranium; timber; gold; oil

CHAD
Total area (sq km): 1,284,000
Total population: 9,826,419
Capital city: N'Djamena
Currency: Communaute Financiere Africaine franc (XAF)
Languages: French; Arabic; Sara; 120 different languages and dialects
Farming (top 5 products): Cotton; sorghum; millet; peanuts; rice
Natural resources (top 5): Oil; uranium; natron; kaolin; fish

COMOROS
Total area (sq km): 2,170
Total population: 671,247
Capital city: Moroni
Currency: Comoran franc (KMF)
Languages: Arabic; French; Shikomoro
Farming (top 5 products): Vanilla; cloves; perfume essences; copra; coconuts
Natural resources: Limited natural resources

CONGO (DEMOCRATIC REPUBLIC OF)
Total area (sq km): 2,345,410
Total population: 60,085,804
Capital city: Kinshasa
Currency: Congolese franc (CDF)

Languages: French; Lingala; Kingwana; Kikongo; Tshiluba
Farming (top 5 products): Coffee; sugar cane; palm oil; rubber; tea
Natural resources (top 5): Cobalt; copper; niobium; tantalum; oil

CONGO (REPUBLIC OF)
Total area (sq km): 342,000
Total population: 3,039,126
Capital city: Brazzaville
Currency: Communaute Financiere Africaine franc (XAF)
Languages: French; Lingala; Monokutuba
Farming (top 5 products): Cassava; sugar cane; rice; corn; peanuts
Natural resources (top 5): Oil; timber; potash; lead; zinc

COTE D'IVOIRE (IVORY COAST)
Total area (sq km): 322,460
Total population: 17,298,040
Capital city: Yamoussoukro/Abidjan
Currency: Communaute Financiere Africaine franc (XOF)
Languages: French; Dioula and 60 indigenous dialects
Farming (top 5 products): Coffee; cocoa; bananas; palm kernels; corn
Natural resources (top 5): Oil; natural gas; diamonds; manganese; iron ore

DJIBOUTI
Total area (sq km): 23,000
Total population: 476,703
Capital city: Djibouti
Currency: Bolivar (VEB)
Languages: French; Arabic; Somali; Afar
Farming: Fruits; vegetables; livestock (including camels)
Natural resources (top 5): Geothermal energy; gold; clay; granite; limestone

An elephant in the Ngorongoro Crater in Tanzania. The Crater is part of *Africa's Great Rift Valley*.

• See the GLOSSARY for words and terms used in these FACTFILES.

AFRICA *Factfiles*

EGYPT
Total area (sq km): 1,001,450
Total population: 77,505,756
Capital city: Cairo
Currency: Egyptian pound (EGP)
Languages: Arabic; English; French
Farming (top 5 products): Cotton; rice; corn; wheat; beans
Natural resources (top 5): Oil; natural gas; iron ore; phosphates; manganese

EQUATORIAL GUINEA
Total area (sq km): 28,051
Total population: 535,881
Capital city: Malabo
Currency: Communaute Financiere Africaine franc (XAF)
Languages: Spanish; French
Farming (top 5 products): Coffee; cocoa; rice; yams; cassava
Natural resources (top 5): Oil; natural gas; timber; gold; bauxite

ERITREA
Total area (sq km): 121,320
Total population: 4,561,599
Capital city: Asmara
Currency: Nafka (ERN)
Languages: Afar; Arabic; Tigre; Kuname; Tigrinya
Farming (top 5 products): Sorghum; lentils; vegetables; corn; cotton
Natural resources (top 5): Gold; potash; zinc; copper; salt

ETHIOPIA
Total area (sq km): 1,127,127
Total population: 75,053,286
Capital city: Addis Ababa
Currency: Birr (ETB)
Languages: Amharic; Tigrinya; Oromigna; Guaragigna; Somali; Arabic
Farming (top 5 products): Cereals; pulses; coffee; oilseed; sugar cane
Natural resources (top 5): Gold; platinum; copper; potash; natural gas

GABON
Total area (sq km): 267,667
Total population: 1,389,201
Capital city: Libreville
Currency: Communaute Financiere Africaine franc (XAF)
Languages: French; Fang; Myene; Nzebi
Farming (top 5 products): Cocoa; coffee; sugar cane; palm oil; rubber
Natural resources (top 5): Oil; natural gas; diamond; niobium; manganese

GAMBIA (THE)
Total area (sq km): 11,300
Total population: 1,593,256
Capital city: Banjul
Currency: Dalasi (GMD)
Languages: English; Mandinka; Wolof
Farming (top 5 products): Rice; millet; sorghum; peanuts; corn
Natural resources (top 5): Fish; titanium; tin; zircon; silica sand

GHANA
Total area (sq km): 239,460
Total population: 21,029,853
Capital city: Accra
Currency: Cedi (GHC)
Languages: Twi; Fante; Ga; Hausa; Dagbani; English
Farming (top 5 products): Cocoa; rice; coffee; cassava; peanuts
Natural resources (top 5): Gold; timber; industrial diamonds; bauxite; manganese

GUINEA
Total area (sq km): 245,857
Total population: 9,467,866
Capital city: Conakry
Currency: Guinean franc (GNF)
Languages: French
Farming (top 5 products): Rice; coffee; pineapples; palm kernels; cassava
Natural resources (top 5): Bauxite; iron ore; diamonds; gold; uranium

GUINEA-BISSAU
Total area (sq km): 36,120
Total population: 1,416,027
Capital city: Bissau
Currency: Communaute Financiere Africaine franc (XOF)
Languages: Crioulo; Balante; Pulaar; Mandjak; Mandinka; Portuguese
Farming (top 5 products): Rice; corn; beans; cassava; cashew nuts
Natural resources (top 5): Fish; timber; phosphates; bauxite; clay

KENYA
Total area (sq km): 582,650
Total population: 33,829,590
Capital city: Nairobi
Currency: Kenyan shilling (KES)
Languages: Swahili; English; Bantu
Farming (top 5 products): Tea; coffee; corn; wheat; sugar cane
Natural resources (top 5): Limestone; soda ash; salt; gemstones; fluorspar

LESOTHO
Total area (sq km): 30,355
Total population: 1,867,035
Capital city: Maseru
Currency: Loti (LSL); South African rand (ZAR)
Languages: Sesotho; English; Zulu; Xhosa
Farming (top 5 products): Corn; wheat; pulses; sorghum; barley
Natural resources (top 5): Diamonds; sand; clay; building stone

LIBERIA
Total area (sq km): 111,370
Total population: 3,482,211
Capital city: Monrovia
Currency: Liberian dollar (LRD)
Languages: Kpelle; English; Bassa
Farming (top 5 products): Rubber; coffee; cocoa; rice; cassava
Natural resources (top 5): Iron ore; timber; diamonds; gold; hydroelectric power

LIBYA
Total area (sq km): 1,759,540
Total population: 5,599,053
Capital city: Tripoli
Currency: Libyan dinar (LYD)
Languages: Arabic; Italian; English
Farming (top 5 products): Wheat; barley; olives; dates; citrus fruits
Natural resources (top 5): Oil; natural gas; gypsum

MADAGASCAR
Total area (sq km): 587,040
Total population: 18,040,341
Capital city: Antananarivo
Currency: Malagasy franc (MGF)
Languages: French; Malagasy
Farming (top 5 products): Coffee; vanilla; sugar cane; cloves; cocoa
Natural resources (top 5): Graphite; chromite; coal; bauxite; salt

MALAWI
Total area (sq km): 118,480
Total population: 12,158,924
Capital city: Lilongwe
Currency: Malawian Kwacha (MWK)
Languages: Chichewa; Chinyanja; Chiyao; Chitumbuka
Farming (top 5 products): Tobacco; sugar cane; cotton; tea; corn
Natural resources: Limestone; hydroelectric power

MALI
Total area (sq km): 1,240,000
Total population: 12,291,529
Capital city: Bamako
Currency: Communaute Financiere Africaine franc (XOF)
Languages: Bambara; Fulani; Songhai; French
Farming (top 5 products): Cotton; millet; rice; corn; vegetables
Natural resources (top 5): Gold; phosphates; kaolin; salt; limestone

MAURITANIA
Total area (sq km): 1,030,700
Total population: 3,086,859
Capital city: Nouakchott
Currency: Ouguiya (MRO)
Languages: Arabic; Pulaar; Soninke; French; Hassaniya; Wolof
Farming (top 5 products): Dates; millet; sorghum; rice; corn
Natural resources (top 5): Iron ore; gypsum; copper; phosphate; diamonds

MAURITIUS
Total area (sq km): 2,040
Total population: 1,230,602
Capital city: Port Louis
Currency: Mauritian rupee (MUR)
Languages: Creole; Bhojpuri; French
Farming (top 5 products): Sugar cane; tea; corn; potatoes; bananas
Natural resources: Fish

MAYOTTE
Total area (sq km): 374
Total population: 193,633
Capital city: Mamoutzou
Currency: Euro (EUR)
Languages: Mahorian; French
Farming: Vanilla; ylang-ylang (perfume essence); coffee; copra
Natural resources: Limited natural resources
Status: French overseas territory

MOROCCO
Total area (sq km): 446,550
Total population: 32,725,847
Capital city: Rabat
Currency: Moroccan dirham (MAD)
Languages: Arabic; Berber dialects; French
Farming (top 5 products): Barley; wheat; citrus fruits; grapes for wine; vegetables
Natural resources (top 5): Phosphates; iron ore; manganese; lead; zinc

• *See the GLOSSARY for words and terms used in these FACTFILES.*

MOZAMBIQUE
Total area (sq km): 801,590
Total population: 19,406,703
Capital city: Maputo
Currency: Metical (MZM)
Languages: Emakhuwa; Xichangana; Portuguese
Farming (top 5 products): Cotton; cashew nuts; sugar cane; tea; cassava
Natural resources (top 5): Coal; titanium; natural gas; hydroelectric power; tantalum

NAMIBIA
Total area (sq km): 825,418
Total population: 2,030,692
Capital city: Windhoek
Currency: Namibian dollar (NAD); South African rand (ZAR)
Languages: English; Afrikaans; German; indigenous languages
Farming: Millet; sorghum; peanuts; livestock
Natural resources (top 5): Diamonds; copper; uranium; gold; lead

NIGER
Total area (sq km): 1,267,000
Total population: 11,665,937
Capital city: Niamey
Currency: Communaute Financiere Africaine franc (XOF)
Languages: French; Hausa; Djerma
Farming (top 5 products): Peas (for cattle feed); cotton; peanuts; millet; sorghum
Natural resources (top 5): Uranium; coal; iron ore; tin; phosphates

NIGERIA
Total area (sq km): 923,768
Total population: 128,771,988
Capital city: Abuja
Currency: Naira (NGN)
Languages: Hausa; Yoruba; Igbo; English; Fulani
Farming (top 5 products): Cocoa; peanuts; palm oil; corn; rice
Natural resources (top 5): Natural gas; oil; tin; iron ore; coal

REUNION
Total area (sq km): 2,517
Total population: 776,948
Capital city: Saint–Denis
Currency: Euro (EUR)
Languages: French; Creole
Farming (top 5 products): Sugar cane; vanilla; tobacco; tropical fruits; vegetables
Natural resources: Fish; hydroelectric power
Status: French overseas territory

RWANDA

Total area (sq km): 26,338
Total population: 8,440,820
Capital city: Kigali
Currency: Rwandan franc (RWF)
Languages: Kinyarwanda; French; English; Kiswahili
Farming (top 5 products): Coffee; tea; pyrethrum; bananas; beans
Natural resources (top 5): Gold; tin ore; tungsten ore; methane; hydroelectric power

SAO TOME AND PRINCIPE
Total area (sq km): 1,001
Total population: 187,410
Capital city: Sao Tome
Currency: Dobra (STD)
Languages: Portuguese
Farming (top 5 products): Cocoa; coconuts; palm kernels; copra; cinnamon
Natural resources: Fish; hydroelectric power

SENEGAL
Total area (sq km): 196,190
Total population: 11,126,832
Capital city: Dakar
Currency: Communaute Financiere Africaine franc (XOF)
Languages: Wolof; French; Pulaar; Jola; Mandinka
Farming (top 5 products): Peanuts; millet; corn; sorghum; rice
Natural resources: Fish; phosphates; iron ore

SEYCHELLES
Total area (sq km): 455
Total population: 81,188
Capital city: Victoria
Currency: Seychelles rupee (SCR)
Languages: Creole; English
Farming (top 5 products): Coconuts; cinnamon; vanilla; sweet potatoes; cassava
Natural resources: Fish; copra; cinnamon trees

SIERRA LEONE
Total area (sq km): 71,740
Total population: 6,017,643
Capital city: Freetown
Currency: Leone (SLL)
Languages: Mende; Temne; Krio; English
Farming (top 5 products): Rice; coffee; cocoa; palm kernels; palm oil
Natural resources (top 5): Diamonds; titanium; bauxite; iron ore; gold

SOMALIA
Total area (sq km): 637,657
Total population: 8,591,629
Capital city: Mogadishu
Currency: Somali shilling (SOS)
Languages: Somali; Arabic; English
Farming (top 5 products): Livestock; bananas; sorghum; corn; coconuts
Natural resources: Uranium; unexploited resources including iron ore, tin, gypsum, bauxite and copper

SOUTH AFRICA
Total area (sq km): 1,219,912
Total population: 44,344,136
Capital city: Pretoria
Currency: Rand (ZAR)
Languages: IsiZulu; IsiXhosa; Afrikaans; Sepedi; English
Farming (top 5 products): Coffee; cotton; sugar cane; rice; potatoes
Natural resources (top 5): Gold; chromium; antimony; coal; iron ore

SUDAN
Total area (sq km): 2,505,810
Total population: 40,187,486
Capital city: Khartoum
Currency: Sudanese dinar (SDD)
Languages: Arabic; English
Farming (top 5 products): Cotton; groundnuts; sorghum; millet; wheat
Natural resources (top 5): Oil; small reserves of iron ore, copper, chromium ore, zinc, tungsten, mica, silver and gold

SWAZILAND

Total area (sq km): 17,363
Total population: 1,173,900
Capital city: Mbabane/Lobamba
Currency: Lilangeni (SZL)
Languages: English; siSwati
Farming (top 5 products): Sugar cane; cotton; corn; tobacco; rice
Natural resources (top 5): Asbestos; coal; clay; cassiterite; hydroelectric power

TANZANIA
Total area (sq km): 945,087
Total population: 36,766,356
Capital city: Dar es Salaam/Dodoma
Currency: Tanzanian shilling (TZS)
Languages: Swahili; Kiunguja; English; Arabic
Farming (top 5 products): Coffee; sisal; tea; cotton; pyrethrum
Natural resources (top 5): Hydroelectric power; tin; phosphates; iron ore; coal

TOGO
Total area (sq km): 56,785
Total population: 5,681,519
Capital city: Lome
Currency: Communaute Financiere Africaine franc (XOF)
Languages: Mina; Ewe; Kabye; Dagomba; French
Farming (top 5 products): Coffee; cocoa; cotton; yams; cassava
Natural resources: Phosphates; limestone; marble

TUNISIA
Total area (sq km): 163,610
Total population: 10,074,951
Capital city: Tunis
Currency: Tunisian dinar (TND)
Languages: Arabic; French
Farming (top 5 products): Olives; olive oil; grain; dairy products; tomatoes
Natural resources (top 5): Oil; phosphates; iron ore; lead; zinc

UGANDA
Total area (sq km): 236,040
Total population: 27,269,482
Capital city: Kampala
Currency: Ugandan shilling (UGX)
Languages: Luganda; English; Swahili
Farming (top 5 products): Coffee; tea; cotton; tobacco; cassava
Natural resources (top 5): Copper; cobalt; hydroelectric power; limestone; salt

ZAMBIA
Total area (sq km): 752,614
Total population: 11,261,795
Capital city: Lusaka
Currency: Zambian kwacha (ZMK)
Languages: Bemba; Tonga; Nyanja; around 70 indigenous languages; English
Farming (top 5 products): Corn; sorghum; rice; peanuts; sunflower seeds
Natural resources (top 5): Copper; cobalt; zinc; lead; coal

ZIMBABWE
Total area (sq km): 390,580
Total population: 12,746,990
Capital city: Harare
Currency: Zimbabwean dollar (ZWD)
Languages: Shona; Ndebele; English
Farming (top 5 products): Corn; cotton; tobacco; wheat; coffee
Natural resources (top 5): Coal; chromium ore; asbestos; gold; nickel

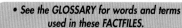
• See the GLOSSARY for words and terms used in these FACTFILES.

EUROPE

PEOPLE FACTFILE

Total population of continent:
800,000,000 (includes total population of the Russian Federation)

Highest population:
Russian Federation 143,420,309

Lowest population:
Vatican City 921

Most populous city:
Moscow, Russia
10,672,000 residents

Average life expectancy:
Male: 73 years
Female: 80 years

Highest infant mortality rate:
Turkey: 41 deaths per 1000 births

> • See the GLOSSARY for definitions of LIFE EXPECTANCY and INFANT MORTALITY RATE.

Average annual income per person:
Highest: Luxembourg £33,170
Lowest: Moldova £1,070

GEOGRAPHY FACTFILE

Total land area:
9,957,000 sq km
(including European Russia)

Largest country in Europe:
European Russia:
4,294,376 sq km
Russia spans the continents of Europe and Asia with its total area divided between both.

Smallest country:
Vatican city: 0.44 sq km

There are no deserts in Europe

Largest lake:
Lake Baykal, Russia
31,000 sq km

Highest waterfall:
Utigard, Norway
Total drop: 800 m

> • See page 44 SIBERIA.
> • See page 41 EUROPE FACTFILES.

Eurasia is one giant landmass, comprising the continents of Europe and Asia. The vast Russian Federation has its capital city, Moscow, in Europe, but spreads for thousands of kilometres across the north of Asia. The landscapes of Europe vary from frozen regions in the Arctic Circle to hot countries bordering the Mediterranean Sea. There are few remaining wilderness areas in Europe, and the continent is criss-crossed by railways and motorways joining large towns and cities.

The giant *Rock of Gibraltar* towers over the *Strait of Gibraltar* which links the Atlantic Ocean and the Mediterranean Sea. The rock is 426 m high.

HIGHEST MOUNTAINS (BY COUNTRY)

NAME	LOCATION	HEIGHT (metres)
Elbrus	Russia	5,642*
Mont Blanc	France/Italy	4,808
Monte Rosa	Italy/Switzerland	4,634
Matterhorn	Italy	4,478

* Elbrus is the highest mountain in Europe.

LONGEST RIVERS

NAME	RIVER MOUTH	LENGTH (km)
Volga	Caspian Sea	3,700
Danube	Black Sea	2,850
Ural	Caspian Sea	2,535
Dnieper	Black Sea	2,285

LARGEST ISLANDS

NAME		AREA (sq km)
Great Britain (mainland)	North Sea/Atlantic Ocean	229,880
Iceland	Atlantic Ocean	103,000
Ireland	Atlantic Ocean	70,280

OIL CONSUMPTION

The amount of oil produced, bought and sold, and used in the world is measured in barrels. A barrel is equivalent to 192 litres.

Russia is Europe's largest producer of oil – 8,420,000 barrels per day.

TOP 5 CONSUMERS OF OIL (USAGE PER DAY)	
Germany	2,891,000 barrels
Russia	2,310,000 barrels
France	2,026,000 barrels
Italy	1,866,000 barrels
UK	1,692,000 barrels

FAST FACTS

• The Vatican City is the smallest state in the world. It covers an area of just 0.44 sq km in the centre of Rome. Vatican City is the headquarters of the Roman Catholic Church.

• Large parts of the Netherlands were once part of the North Sea. Long embankments called *dykes* have been built to hold back the ocean and parts of the coast have been reclaimed and pumped dry. These areas are called *polders*.

• The city of Venice in Italy is made up of 117 small islands that were built hundreds of years ago on salt marshes. The islands are joined to each other by 409 bridges. There are 150 seawater canals running between the islands. Workers, residents and visitors travel around the city by boat.

• The coast of the United Kingdom has so many indents it means that no point in the UK is more than 113 km from the sea.

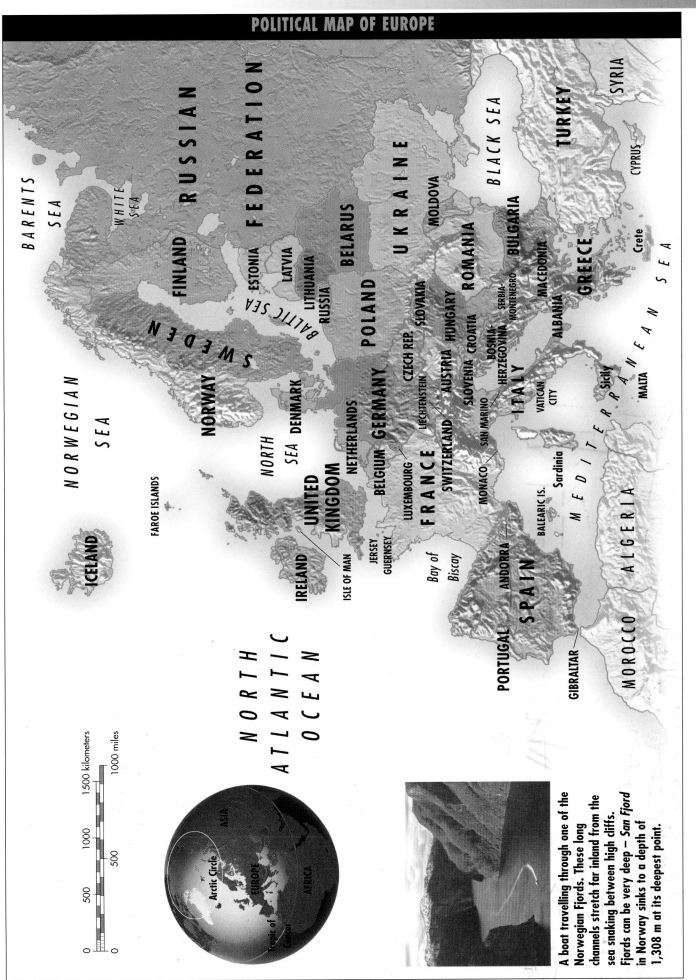

BARENTS SEA

WHITE SEA

NORWEGIAN SEA

NORTH ATLANTIC OCEAN

FINLAND

RUSSIAN FEDERATION

SWEDEN

NORWAY

ICELAND

FAROE ISLANDS

ESTONIA
LATVIA
LITHUANIA
RUSSIA

BALTIC SEA

BELARUS

POLAND

UKRAINE

MOLDOVA

BLACK SEA

TURKEY

SYRIA

CYPRUS

NORTH SEA

DENMARK

NETHERLANDS

UNITED KINGDOM

IRELAND

ISLE OF MAN

JERSEY
GUERNSEY

BELGIUM GERMANY

LUXEMBOURG

CZECH REP.

SLOVAKIA

AUSTRIA HUNGARY

LIECHTENSTEIN

SWITZERLAND

SLOVENIA CROATIA

ROMANIA

BOSNIA-HERZEGOVINA

SERBIA

MONTENEGRO

BULGARIA

MACEDONIA

ALBANIA

GREECE

Crete

FRANCE

SAN MARINO

MONACO

ITALY

VATICAN CITY

Sardinia

Sicily

MALTA

M E D I T E R R A N E A N   S E A

Bay of Biscay

BALEARIC IS.

ANDORRA

PORTUGAL

SPAIN

GIBRALTAR

MOROCCO

ALGERIA

500
1000
1500 kilometers

500
1000 miles

0

ASIA

Arctic Circle

EUROPE

AFRICA

Tropic of Cancer

A boat travelling through one of the Norwegian Fjords. These long channels stretch far inland from the sea snaking between high cliffs. Fjords can be very deep — *San Fjord* in Norway sinks to a depth of 1,308 m at its deepest point.

ICELAND

Bjargtangar · Horn · Akureyri · Fontur
Vatnajökull
REYKJAVÍK · Höfn
Vík

Føroyar
(Faroe Is)
(Denmark)
Tórshavn

Mosjøen
STORUMAN
Skellefte
Trondheimsfjorden
Östersund
Umeå
Trondheim
Storsjön
Sundsvall
Ålesund
Dombås
Hudiksvall
Sagnefjorden
Gävle
Åland
Bergen
OSLO
Karlstad
Mälaren
Uppsala
Shetland Is
Drammen
Örebro
STOCKHOLM
Stavanger
Arendal
Vänern
Vättern
Gotland
Orkney Is
Kristiansand
Jönköping
Göteburg
Skagerrak
Liep
Hebrides
Inverness
North
Sea
Ålborg
DENMARK
Helsingborg
Kaliningrad
Aberdeen
Esbjerg
KØBENHAVN
Malmö
Glasgow
Edinburgh
Odense
Sjælland
Gdańsk
Londonderry
UNITED
Newcastle upon Tyne
Kiel
Rügen
Rostock
Szczecin
Bydgoszcz
Belfast
ISLE OF
MAN
Leeds
Kingston upon Hull
Hamburg
NETHER-
LANDS
Bremen
BERLIN
Poznań
Łódź
Galway
DUBLIN
Irish
Sea
Liverpool
Norwich
AMSTERDAM
Hannover
POLA
REP. OF
IRELAND
KINGDOM
Birmingham
's-GRAVENHAGE
GERMANY
Cork
Cardiff
Bristol
Rotterdam
Düsseldorf
Dresden
Wrocław
Celtic
Sea
LONDON
BRUSSELS
Frankfurt
PRAHA
(PRAGUE)
CZECH
REPUBLIC
Ostrava
Kra
Southampton
Brighton
BELGIUM
LUXEMBOURG
LUX.
Nürnberg
Brno
Plymouth
English Channel
GUERNSEY
JERSEY
Le Havre
Seine
PARIS
Strasbourg
Stuttgart
WIEN
(VIENNA)
SLOVAKIA
BRATISLAVA
BUDA
Brest
Rennes
Dijon
Zürich
VADUZ
LIECH.
Salzburg
AUSTRIA
Graz
Győr
HUNGARY
Loire
Lyon
BERN
SWITZERLAND
Mont Blanc
4808
Matterhorn
4478
Milano
Venezia
SLOVENIA
LJUBLJANA
ZAGREB
Pécs
FRANCE
Limoges
Torino
Po
Bologna
CROATIA
BOSNIA-
HERTZ.
Nantes
Bordeaux
Garonne
Montpellier
Nice
Genova
Firenze
SAN
MARINO
SARAJEVO
SERB
&
MON
Rhône
MONACO
Bay of
Biscay
A Coruña
Gijón
Bilbao
ANDORRA
Gulf du
Lion
Marseille
Corse
Ajaccio
VATICAN
CITY
ITALY
Pescara
Adriatic Sea
TIRANË
ALBANIA
Cabo Fisterra
Pamplona
Pyrenees
Zaragoza
Barcelona
ROMA
(ROME)
Bari
Plain
Vigo
Vallodolid
Ebro
Sássari
Napoli
Taranto
Kerkyra
Porto
MADRID
Islas Baleares
Menorca
Mallorca
Sardegna
Tyrrhenian
Sea
Coimbra
SPAIN
Palma
Eivissa
Cagliari
Palermo
Messina
Ionian
Sea
PORTUGAL
Badajoz
Valencia
Mediter
Sicilia
Etna 3323
LISBOA
(LISBON)
Córdoba
Alicante
Cartagena
ALGER
(ALGIERS)
Siracusa
Cabo
de São Vicente
Faro
Sevilla
Mulbacén
3482
Annaba
VALLETTA
MALTA
Tanger
Gibraltar (U.K.)
Sidi Bel
Abbès
TUNIS
ranea
RABAT
Fès
Sfax
TUNI
Golfe de Gabès
a

N
W E
S

Donegal Bay
Celtic Shelf

Celtic
Sea

Gulf of

Baltic Sea

Cabo
de São Vicente

38

PHYSICAL MAP OF EUROPE

Miller Cylindrical Projection

■ Capital city
■ Administrative capital
● Other city or town
▲ Mountain summit (heights in metres)
〰 Dry salt lake
〰 Marsh
— International boundary
······· International boundary, disputed
----- Administrative boundary

Land heights metres	Sea depths metres
8000	500
7000	1000
6000	2000
5000	4000
4000	5000
3000	6000
2000	7000
1000	
500	
200	
0	
Land below sea level	

Gällivare
Rovaniemi
Boden
Kemi
Oulu
FINLAND
Ozero Topozero
White
Se
Vaasa
Kajaani
Lieksa
Kuopio
Ozero Vygozero
Jyväskylä
Pori
Tampere
Orivesi
Petrozavodsk
Onez Ozero
Saimaa
Turku
Ladozhskoye Ozero
HELSINKI
Vyborg
Gulf of Finland
Sankt-Peterburg
Ozero Beloye
Cherepovets
Vologda
TALLINN
Kingisepp
RUSSIAN
ESTONIA
Tartu
Velikiy Novgorod
Rybinskoye Vodokhranilishche
Kotel'nich
Kirov
Lake Peipus
Ozero Il'men'
Kostroma
FEDERATION
Ventspils
Valmiera
Pskov
Yaroslavl'
Ivanovo
Nizhniy-Novgorod
Izhevsk
pa
RĪGA
LATVIA
Rēzekne
Velikiye Luki
Tver'
Vladimir
Volga
Kazan'
Naberez
Chelny
Šiauliai
Daugavpils
MOSKVA
(MOSCOW)
Murom
Arzamas
Dimitrovgrad
LITHUANIA
VILNIUS
Vitsyebsk
Smolensk
Kaluga
Ryazan'
Ul'yanovsk
RUS.
FED.
Kaunas
Mahilyow
Tula
Penza
Syzran'
Samara
Hrodna
MINSK
Bryansk
Orel
Tambov
Volga
Białystok
BELARUS
Klintsy
Lipetsk
Saratov
Balakovo
WARSZAWA
Brest
Homyel
Kursk
Voronezh
Ura
ND
Lublin
Korosten'
Chernihiv
Belgorod
Kamyshin
Ural'sk
ców
Rivne
KYIV
(KIEV)
Sumy
Kharkiv
Volgograd
L'viv
UKRAINE
Poltava
Kamyshin
Akhtubinsk
Zhytomyr
Cherkasy
Dnipropetrovs'k
Luhans'k
Atyrau
Carpathian Mts
Vinnytsya
Kryvyy
Rih
Zaporizhzhya
Donets'k
Volgodonsk
Volga
Uzhorod
MOLDOVA
Rostov-na-Donu
Astrakhan
K
EST
Oradea
CHIŞINĂU
Iaşi
Mykolayiv
Mariupol'
Elista
Aktau
Arad
Cluj-Napoca
Odesa
Sea of Azov
Krasnodar
ROMANIA
Kerch
Stavropol'
Caspian Sea
vi Sad
Braşov
Sevastopol'
Sudak
Maykop
Nevinnomyssk
Zaliv Kara-Gol
BEOGRAD
(BELGRADE)
BUCUREŞTI
(BUCHAREST)
Constanţa
Elbrus 5642
Nal'chik
Aktau
BIA
Craiova
Danube
Black Sea
Sokhumi
Groznyy
Niš
BULGARIA
Varna
Makhachkala
TE.
SOFIYA
Burgas
Sinop
K'ut'aisi
GEORGIA
SKOPJE
Edirne
İstanbul
Samsun
Bat'umi
T'BILISI
Gäncä
BAKI
Turkm
MAC.
Zonguldak
Çorum
Trabzon
Gyumri
AZERBAIJAN
Thessaloníki
Sakarya
Bursa
Sivas
YEREVAN
ARMENIA
Äli Bayrami
Larisa
Aegean Sea
ANKARA
Erzurum
Ararat 5165
Xankändi
Nebitdag
GREECE
İzmir
TURKEY
AZER.
Lake Van
Tabrīz
Ardabīl
ATHINA
(ATHENS)
Isparta
Konya
Kahramanmaraş
Van
Orūmīyeh
Tripoli
Antalya
Adana
Al Hasakah
Damāvand 5604
atra
Ródos
Dodekanisos
Al Lādhiqīyah
Ḩalab
Ar Raqqah
TEHRĀN
Elburz
Chania
Rodos
LEFKOSIA
(NICOSIA)
Ḩamāh
Tarṭūs
SYRIA
Qom
Das
Kriti (Crete)
Iraklion
CYPRUS
LEBANON
Ḩimş
Euphrates
Tigris
Kermānshāh
a
DIMASHQ
BEIRUT

HABITATS: EUROPE

This map shows the different types of habitat across the continent.

HABITATS KEY

- Ice and snow
- Tundra
- Mountains/barren land
- Forest
- Grassland
- Semidesert
- Desert

THE EUROPEAN UNION

The European Union (EU) is an organisation set up to allow European countries to band together to support each other.

WHAT DOES THE EU DO?

The EU has set up laws which protect EU workers, help member countries trade easily and allow EU workers to work in any other EU country without permits or visas.

THE EEC

The organisation began in 1957. Six European countries formed the European Economic Community (EEC) with the aim of abolishing tariffs and trading restrictions between members. The countries were Belgium, France, Germany, Italy, Luxembourg and the Netherlands.

THE EU

More European countries joined the group and in 1992, the organisation became the EU. Member states agreed to work together in many areas including defence, foreign policy and social policies.

Today 25 European countries are members of the European Union.

EUROPEAN UNION MEMBERS

The 25 EU member states and the year they joined the Union:

Belgium	1957	Greece	1981	Poland	2004
France	1957	Spain	1986	Czech Republic	2004
Germany	1957	Portugal	1986	Slovakia	2004
Italy	1957	Austria	1995	Hungary	2004
Luxembourg	1957	Finland	1995	Slovenia	2004
The Netherlands	1957	Sweden	1995	Malta	2004
Denmark	1973	Estonia	2004	Cyprus	2004
Ireland	1973	Latvia	2004		
United Kingdom	1973	Lithuania	2004		

LAND USE

- **Forest** including trees grown for timber
- **Permanent pasture**
- **Permanent crops** such as fruit trees or grapevines
- **Arable** crops such as wheat and rice which are replanted each year
- **Other** – roads, towns and barren land

32.5%
46%
12.8%
8%
0.7%

EU FLAG AND THE EURO

The European Union flag has 12 stars for the 12 countries who were members when the EU was named in 1992.

- EU member countries have an EU FLAG in the EUROPE FACTFILES which begin on page 41.

Total population of 25 EU member states:

457,000,000

Total area of EU zone:

3,976,372 sq km

The *Euro* was launched as a unit of exchange throughout the European Union on 1 January, 1999.

The euro is used by 12 EU countries as their currency: Austria, Belgium, Finland, France, Germany, Greece, Ireland, Italy, Luxembourg, Netherlands, Portugal and Spain.

CLIMATE: EUROPE

CLIMATES KEY

- over 32°C
- 24° to 32°C
- 15° to 24°C
- 7° to 15°C
- –1° to 7°C
- –9° to –1°C
- –18° to –9°C
- –23° to –18°C
- below –23°C

TEMPERATURES IN JANUARY

ARCTIC CIRCLE

TEMPERATURES IN JULY

ARCTIC CIRCLE

EUROPE FACTFILES

Each country by country factfile contains: **total area** of the country in square kilometres; **total population**; name of the **capital city**; the main **currency** used in the country; **main languages spoken** (listed in order of number of speakers); **top five farming products produced** (listed in order of importance to the country's economy); **natural resources** (of commercial importance); and a country's **status** if it is not independent.

ALBANIA

Total area (sq km): 28,748
Total population: 3,563,112
Capital city: Tirana
Currency: Lek (ALL)
Languages: Albanian; Greek, Vlach
Farming (top 5 products): Wheat; corn; potatoes; vegetables; fruit
Natural resources (top 5): Oil; natural gas; coal; bauxite; chromite

ANDORRA
Total area (sq km): 468
Total population: 70,549
Capital city: Andorra la Vella
Currency: Euro (EUR)
Languages: Catalan; French; Castilian; Portuguese
Farming (top 5 products): Rye; wheat; barley; oats; vegetables
Natural resources (top 5): Hydroelectric power; mineral water; timber; iron ore; lead

AUSTRIA
Total area (sq km): 83,870
Total population: 8,184,691
Capital city: Vienna
Currency: Euro (EUR)
Languages: German; Slovene; Croatian; Hungarian
Farming (top 5 products): Cereal crops; potatoes; sugar beets; grapes for wine; fruit
Natural resources (top 5): Oil; coal; lignite; timber; iron ore

BELARUS

Total area (sq km): 207,600
Total population: 10,300,483
Capital city: Minsk
Currency: Belarussian ruble (BYB/BYR)
Languages: Belarussian; Russian
Farming (top 5 products): Cereal crops; potatoes; vegetables; sugar beets; flax
Natural resources (top 5): Timber; peat; small quantities oil and natural gas; granite; limestone

BELGIUM
Total area (sq km): 30,528
Total population: 10,364,388
Capital city: Brussels
Currency: Euro (EUR)
Languages: Dutch; French; German
Farming (top 5 products): Sugar beets; vegetables; fruit; cereal crops; tobacco
Natural resources: Construction materials; silica sand; carbonates

BOSNIA–HERZEGOVINA

Total area (sq km): 51,129
Total population: 4,025,476
Capital city: Sarajevo
Currency: Marka (BAM)
Languages: Bosnian; Croatian; Serbian
Farming (top 5 products): Wheat; corn; fruits; vegetables; livestock
Natural resources (top 5): Coal; iron ore; bauxite; copper; lead

BULGARIA
Total area (sq km): 110,910
Total population: 7,450,349
Capital city: Sofia
Currency: Lev (BGL)
Languages: Bulgarian; Turkish; Roma
Farming (top 5 products): Vegetables; fruit; tobacco; livestock; grapes for wine
Natural resources (top 5): Bauxite; copper; lead; zinc; coal

CROATIA
Total area (sq km): 56,542
Total population: 4,495,904
Capital city: Zagreb
Currency: Kuna (HRK)
Languages: Croatian; Serbian
Farming (top 5 products): Wheat; corn; sugar beets; sunflower seeds; barley
Natural resources (top 5): Oil; coal; bauxite; iron ore; calcium

CYPRUS

Total area (sq km): 9,250
Total population: 780,133
Capital city: Nicosia
Currency: Cypriot pound (CYP); Turkish lira (TRL)
Languages: Greek; Turkish; English
Farming (top 5 products): Citrus fruits; vegetables; barley; grapes; olives
Natural resources (top 5): Copper; pyrites; asbestos; gypsum; timber

CZECH REPUBLIC

Total area (sq km): 78,866
Total population: 10,241,138
Capital city: Prague
Currency: Czech koruna (CZK)
Languages: Czech
Farming (top 5 products): Wheat; potatoes; sugar beets; hops; fruit
Natural resources (top 5): Coal; kaolin; clay; graphite; timber

DENMARK

Total area (sq km): 43,094
Total population: 5,432,335
Capital city: Copenhagen
Currency: Danish krone (DKK)
Languages: Danish; Faroese; Greenlandic; German
Farming (top 5 products): Barley; wheat; potatoes; sugar beets; pigs
Natural resources (top 5): Oil; natural gas; fish; salt; limestone

ESTONIA

Total area (sq km): 45,226
Total population: 1,332,893
Capital city: Tallinn
Currency: Estonian kroon (EEK)
Languages: Estonian; Russian
Farming: Potatoes; vegetables; livestock; dairy products
Natural resources (top 5): Oil shale; peat; phosphorite; clay; limestone

FAROE ISLANDS

Total area (sq km): 1,399
Total population: 49,962
Capital city: Caracas
Currency: Danish krone (DKK)
Languages: Faroese; Danish
Farming (top 5 products): Milk; potatoes; vegetables; sheep; salmon
Natural resources: Fish; whales; hydroelectric power
Status: Self-governing Danish territory

FINLAND

Total area (sq km): 338,145
Total population: 5,223,442
Capital city: Helsinki
Currency: Euro (EUR)
Languages: Finnish; Swedish
Farming (top 5 products): Barley; wheat; sugar beets; potatoes; cattle
Natural resources (top 5): Timber; iron ore; copper; lead; zinc

FRANCE
Total area (sq km): 547,030
Total population: 60,656,178
Capital city: Paris
Currency: Euro (EUR)
Languages: French
Farming (top 5 products): Wheat; cereal crops; sugar beets; potatoes; grapes for wine
Natural resources (top 5): Coal; iron ore; bauxite; zinc; uranium

• See the GLOSSARY for words and terms used in these FACTFILES.

EUROPE *Factfiles*

GERMANY

Total area (sq km): 357,021
Total population: 82,431,390
Capital city: Berlin
Currency: Euro (EUR)
Languages: German
Farming (top 5 products): Potatoes; wheat; barley; sugar beets; fruit
Natural resources (top 5): Coal; lignite; natural gas; iron ore; copper

GIBRALTAR
Total area (sq km): 6.5
Total population: 27,884
Capital city: Gibraltar
Currency: Gibraltar pound (GIP)
Languages: English; Spanish; Italian; Portuguese
Farming: No farming
Natural resources: No natural resources
Status: United Kingdom overseas territory

GREECE
Total area (sq km): 131,940
Total population: 10,668,354
Capital city: Athens
Currency: Euro (EUR)
Languages: Greek
Farming (top 5 products): Wheat; corn; barley; sugar beets; olives
Natural resources (top 5): Lignite; oil; iron ore; bauxite; lead

GUERNSEY
Total area (sq km): 78
Total population: 65,228
Capital city: Saint Peter Port
Currency: British pound (GBP)
Languages: English; French
Farming (top 5 products): Tomatoes; cut flowers; sweet peppers; aubergines; fruit
Natural resources: Arable land
Status: United Kingdom Crown Dependency

HUNGARY
Total area (sq km): 93,030
Total population: 10,006,835
Capital city: Budapest
Currency: Forint (HUF)
Languages: Hungarian
Farming (top 5 products): Wheat; corn; sunflower seeds; potatoes; sugar beets
Natural resources: Bauxite; coal; natural gas

ICELAND
Total area (sq km): 103,000
Total population: 296,737
Capital city: Reykjavik
Currency: Icelandic krona (ISK)
Languages: Icelandic; English
Farming: Potatoes; vegetables; sheep; dairy products
Natural resources: Fish; hydroelectric power; geothermal power

IRELAND
Total area (sq km): 70,280
Total population: 4,015,676
Capital city: Dublin
Currency: Euro (EUR)
Languages: English; Irish (Gaelic/Gaeilge)
Farming (top 5 products): Turnips; barley; potatoes; sugar beets; wheat
Natural resources (top 5): Natural gas; peat; copper; lead; zinc

ISLE OF MAN
Total area (sq km): 572
Total population: 75,049
Capital city: Douglas
Currency: British pound (GBP)
Languages: English; Manx Gaelic
Farming: Cereal crops; vegetables; livestock; poultry
Natural resources: No natural resources
Status: United Kingdom Crown Dependency

ITALY
Total area (sq km): 301,230
Total population: 58,103,033
Capital city: Rome
Currency: Euro (EUR)
Languages: Italian
Farming (top 5 products): Fruit; vegetables; grapes for wine; potatoes; sugar beets
Natural resources (top 5): Coal; mercury; zinc; potash; marble

JERSEY
Total area (sq km): 116
Total population: 90,812
Capital city: Saint Helier
Currency: British pound (GBP)
Languages: English
Farming (top 5 products): Potatoes; cauliflower; tomatoes; cattle; dairy products
Natural resources: Arable land
Status: United Kingdom Crown Dependency

LATVIA
Total area (sq km): 64,589
Total population: 2,290,237
Capital city: Riga
Currency: Latvian lat (LVL)
Languages: Latvian; Russian
Farming (top 5 products): Cereal crops; sugar beets; potatoes; vegetables; livestock
Natural resources (top 5): Peat; limestone; dolomite; amber; hydroelectric power

LIECHTENSTEIN
Total area (sq km): 160
Total population: 33,717
Capital city: Vaduz
Currency: Swiss franc (CHF)
Languages: German
Farming (top 5 products): Wheat; barley; corn; potatoes; livestock
Natural resources: hydroelectric power potential; arable land

LITHUANIA
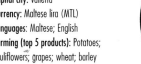
Total area (sq km): 65,200
Total population: 3,596,617
Capital city: Vilnius
Currency: Litas (LTL)
Languages: Lithuanian; Russian
Farming (top 5 products): Cereal crops; potatoes; sugar beets; flax; vegetables
Natural resources: Peat; arable land

LUXEMBOURG
Total area (sq km): 2,586
Total population: 468,571
Capital city: Luxembourg
Currency: Euro (EUR)
Languages: Luxembourgish; German; French
Farming (top 5 products): Barley; oats; potatoes; wheat; fruit
Natural resources: Arable land

MACEDONIA

Total area (sq km): 25,333
Total population: 2,045,262
Capital city: Skopje
Currency: Macedonian denar (MKD)
Languages: Macedonian; Albanian
Farming (top 5 products): Wheat; grapes; rice; tobacco; corn
Natural resources (top 5): Iron ore; copper; lead; zinc; chromite

MALTA

Total area (sq km): 316
Total population: 398,534
Capital city: Valletta
Currency: Maltese lira (MTL)
Languages: Maltese; English
Farming (top 5 products): Potatoes; cauliflowers; grapes; wheat; barley
Natural resources: Limestone; salt; arable land

MOLDOVA

Total area (sq km): 33,843
Total population: 4,455,421
Capital city: Chisinau
Currency: Moldovan leu (MDL)
Languages: Moldovan; Russian; Gagauz (a Turkish dialect)
Farming (top 5 products): Vegetables; fruit; grapes for wine; cereal crops; sugar beets
Natural resources: Lignite; phosphorites; gypsum

MONACO
Total area (sq km): 1.95
Total population: 32,409
Capital city: Monaco
Currency: Euro (EUR)
Languages: French; English; Italian; Monegasque
Farming: No farming
Natural resources: No natural resources

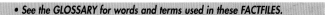

• See the GLOSSARY for words and terms used in these FACTFILES.

NETHERLANDS

Total area (sq km): 41,526
Total population: 16,407,491
Capital city: Amsterdam
Currency: Euro (EUR)
Languages: Dutch; Frisian
Farming (top 5 products): Cereal crops; potatoes; sugar beets; fruit; vegetables
Natural resources (top 5): Natural gas; oil; peat; limestone; salt

NORWAY

Total area (sq km): 324,220
Total population: 4,593,041
Capital city: Oslo
Currency: Norwegian krone (NOK)
Languages: Bokmal Norwegian; Nynorsk Norwegian; small Sami and Finnish-speaking minorities
Farming (top 5 products): Barley; wheat; potatoes; livestock; milk
Natural resources (top 5): Oil; natural gas; iron ore; copper; lead

POLAND

Total area (sq km): 312,685
Total population: 38,635,144
Capital city: Warsaw
Currency: Zloty (PLN)
Languages: Polish
Farming (top 5 products): Potatoes; fruit; vegetables; wheat; poultry
Natural resources (top 5): Coal; sulphur; copper; natural gas; silver

PORTUGAL

Total area (sq km): 92,391
Total population: 10,566,212
Capital city: Lisbon
Currency: Euro (EUR)
Languages: Portuguese; Mirandese
Farming (top 5 products): Cereal crops; potatoes; olives; grapes; livestock
Natural resources (top 5): Fish; cork forests; iron ore; copper; zinc

ROMANIA

Total area (sq km): 237,500
Total population: 22,329,977
Capital city: Bucharest
Currency: Leu (ROL)
Languages: Romanian; Hungarian; German
Farming (top 5 products): Wheat; corn; barley; sugar beets; sunflower seeds
Natural resources (top 5): Oil; timber; natural gas; coal; iron ore

RUSSIAN FEDERATION

Total area (sq km): 17,075,200
Total population: 143,420,309
Capital city: Moscow
Currency: Russian ruble (RUR)
Languages: Russian
Farming (top 5 products): Cereal crops; sugar beets; sunflower seeds; vegetables; fruit
Natural resources (top 5): Oil; natural gas; coal; many minerals; timber

SAN MARINO

Total area (sq km): 61.2
Total population: 28,880
Capital city: San Marino
Currency: Euro (EUR)
Languages: Italian
Farming (top 5 products): Wheat; grapes; corn; olives; livestock
Natural resources: Stone for construction

SERBIA MONTENEGRO

Total area (sq km): 102,350
Total population: 10,829,175
Capital city: Belgrade
Currency: Yugoslav dinar (YUM); Euro (EUR)
Languages: Serbian; Albanian
Farming (top 5 products): Coffee; cotton; sugar cane; rice; potatoes
Natural resources (top 5): Oil; gas; coal; iron ore; bauxite

SLOVAKIA

Total area (sq km): 48,845
Total population: 5,431,363
Capital city: Bratislava
Currency: Slovak koruna (SKK)
Languages: Slovak; Hungarian
Farming (top 5 products): Cereal crops; potatoes; sugar beets; hops; fruit
Natural resources (top 5): Coal; lignite; iron ore; copper; manganese

SLOVENIA

Total area (sq km): 20,273
Total population: 2,011,070
Capital city: Ljubljana
Currency: Tolar (SIT)
Languages: Slovenian; Serbo-Croatian
Farming (top 5 products): Potatoes; hops; wheat; sugar beets; corn
Natural resources (top 5): Lignite; lead; zinc; mercury; uranium

SPAIN

Total area (sq km): 504,782
Total population: 40,341,462
Capital city: Madrid
Currency: Euro (EUR)
Languages: Castilian Spanish; Catalan; Galician; Basque
Farming (top 5 products): Cereal crops; vegetables; olives; grapes for wine; sugar beets
Natural resources (top 5): Coal; lignite; iron ore; copper; lead

SWEDEN

Total area (sq km): 449,964
Total population: 9,001,774
Capital city: Stockholm
Currency: Swedish krona (SEK)
Languages: Swedish; small Sami and Finnish-speaking minorities
Farming (top 5 products): Barley; wheat; sugar beets; livestock; milk
Natural resources (top 5): Iron ore; copper; lead; zinc; gold

SWITZERLAND

Total area (sq km): 41,290
Total population: 7,489,370
Capital city: Bern
Currency: Swiss franc (CHF)
Languages: German; French; Italian
Farming (top 5 products): Cereal crops; fruit; vegetables; livestock; eggs
Natural resources: Hydroelectric power potential; timber; salt

TURKEY

Total area (sq km): 780,580
Total population: 69,660,559
Capital city: Ankara
Currency: New Turkish lira (YTL)
Languages: Turkish; Kurdish; Arabic; Armenian; Greek
Farming (top 5 products): Tobacco; cotton; cereals; olives; sugar beets
Natural resources (top 5): Coal; iron ore; copper; chromium; antimony

UKRAINE

Total area (sq km): 603,700
Total population: 47,425,336
Capital city: Kiev
Currency: Hryvnia (UAH)
Languages: Ukrainian; Russian
Farming (top 5 products): Cereal crops; sugar beets; sunflower seeds; vegetables; cattle
Natural resources (top 5): Iron ore; coal; manganese; natural gas; oil

UNITED KINGDOM

Total area (sq km): 244,820
Total population: 60,441,457
Capital city: London
Currency: British pound (GBP)
Languages: English
Farming (top 5 products): Cereal crops; oilseed; potatoes; vegetables; livestock
Natural resources (top 5): Coal; oil; natural gas; iron ore; lead

VATICAN CITY

Total area (sq km): 0.44
Total population: 921
Capital city: Vatican City
Currency: Euro (EUR)
Languages: Italian; Latin
Farming: No farming
Natural resources: No natural resources

The Alps mountain range stretches from France, through Switzerland, Liechtenstein and Italy, to Austria and Slovenia. The range is 1,200 km long with a width of 200 km at its widest sections.

• See the GLOSSARY for words and terms used in these FACTFILES.

ASIA

Asia is the world's largest continent, and includes many vast countries, such as the Russian Federation, and countries with huge populations, such as China and India. The landscape includes Arctic tundra, tropical rainforests, and the world's highest mountains, the Himalayas. Rice is Asia's most important food crop and paddy fields can be seen dotted across Southeast Asia – one fifth of the world's rice is grown in this part of Asia.

A worldwide symbol of conservation, China's Giant Panda lives in the mountainous forests of southwestern China.

PEOPLE FACTFILE

Total population of continent:
3,840,000,000 (Does not include population of Russian Federation.)

Highest population:
China 1,306,313,812

Lowest population:
Maldives 349,106

Most populous city in Asia and the world:
Tokyo, Japan 35,327,000 residents

Average life expectancy:
Male: 67 years
Female: 72 years

Highest infant mortality rate:
Afghanistan:
163 deaths per 1000 births

• See the GLOSSARY for definitions of LIFE EXPECTANCY and INFANT MORTALITY RATE.

Average annual income per person:
Highest: Hong Kong £19,260
Lowest: East Timor £225

GEOGRAPHY FACTFILE

Total land area:
44,500,000 sq km
(including Asian Russia)

Largest countries:
Asian Russia:
12,780,824 sq km
China: 9,596,960 sq km

Smallest country:
Macau: 25.4 sq km

Highest mountain in Asia and the world:
Mt Everest, China/Nepal
8,850 m

Longest river:
Yangtze: 6,380 km

Largest dessert:
Arabian Desert, Arabian Peninsula
2,331,000 sq km

Highest waterfall:
Jog Falls, India
Total drop: 253 m

• See page 49 ASIA FACTFILES.

HIGHEST MOUNTAINS (BY COUNTRY)

• See page 10 WORLD'S 10 HIGHEST MOUNTAIN PEAKS for information on Asia's highest mountains.

NAME	LOCATION	HEIGHT (metres)
Qullai Ismoili Somoni	Tajikistan	7,490
Damavand	Iran	5,604
Punkak Jaya	Indonesia	5,030
Kinabalu	Borneo, Malaysia	4,094
Fuji San	Japan	3,776

LARGEST LAKES

NAME		AREA (sq km)
Caspian Sea	Asia	371,000*
Aral Sea	Kazakhstan/Uzbekistan	28,687
Lake Balqash	Kazakhstan	18,500
Ysyk Kol	Kyrgyzstan	6,200

* The Caspian Sea is the world's largest lake.

LARGEST ISLANDS

NAME		AREA (sq km)
Borneo	Southeast Asia	744,360
Sumatra	Indonesia	473,600
Honshu	Japan	227,898

• See page 10 WORLD'S 10 LONGEST RIVERS.

OIL CONSUMPTION

The amount of oil produced, bought and sold, and used in the world is measured in barrels. A barrel is equivalent to 192 litres.

Saudi Arabia is the world's largest producer of oil – 9,021,000 barrels each day.

25% of the world's proven oil reserves are in Saudi Arabia.

TOP 5 CONSUMERS OF OIL IN ASIA (USAGE PER DAY)

Japan	5,290,000 barrels
China	4,956,000 barrels
India	2,130,000 barrels
South Korea	2,070,000 barrels
Saudi Arabia	1,550,000 barrels

SIBERIA

The Russian Federation covers around 11% of the Earth's surface.

• Around 13 million sq km of the country form the great barren plains, tundra regions and taiga forests of Siberia.

• The Trans-Siberian railway is the longest stretch of railway track in the world. The 9,300-kilometre journey from Moscow to Vladivostok (on the Pacific coast) takes around eight days.

POLITICAL MAP OF ASIA

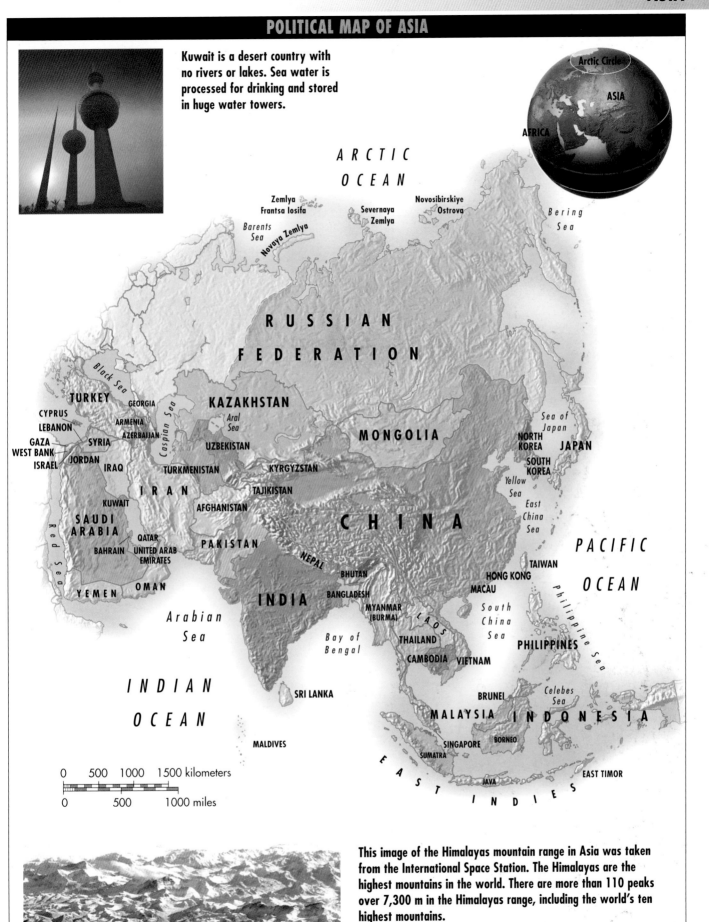

Kuwait is a desert country with no rivers or lakes. Sea water is processed for drinking and stored in huge water towers.

ARCTIC OCEAN

Zemlya Frantsa Iosifa

Severnaya Zemlya

Novosibirskiye Ostrova

Bering Sea

Barents Sea

Novaya Zemlya

RUSSIAN FEDERATION

Black Sea

TURKEY

GEORGIA

Caspian Sea

KAZAKHSTAN

Aral Sea

MONGOLIA

Sea of Japan

CYPRUS
LEBANON

ARMENIA
AZERBAIJAN

NORTH KOREA

JAPAN

GAZA
WEST BANK
ISRAEL

SYRIA
JORDAN
IRAQ

UZBEKISTAN

SOUTH KOREA

I R A N

TURKMENISTAN

KYRGYZSTAN

Yellow Sea

TAJIKISTAN

East China Sea

KUWAIT

AFGHANISTAN

C H I N A

SAUDI ARABIA

QATAR

PACIFIC

BAHRAIN
UNITED ARAB EMIRATES

PAKISTAN

NEPAL

TAIWAN

OCEAN

Red Sea

BHUTAN

HONG KONG
MACAU

YEMEN
OMAN

BANGLADESH

INDIA

MYANMAR (BURMA)

South China Sea

Arabian Sea

Bay of Bengal

LAOS

PHILIPPINES

Philippine Sea

THAILAND

CAMBODIA **VIETNAM**

I N D I A N

SRI LANKA

BRUNEI

Celebes Sea

OCEAN

MALAYSIA **I N D O N E S I A**

MALDIVES

SINGAPORE BORNEO

SUMATRA

E A S T

JAVA

EAST TIMOR

I N D I E S

| 0 | 500 | 1000 | 1500 kilometers |

| 0 | 500 | 1000 miles |

ASIA

AFRICA

Arctic Circle

This image of the Himalayas mountain range in Asia was taken from the International Space Station. The Himalayas are the highest mountains in the world. There are more than 110 peaks over 7,300 m in the Himalayas range, including the world's ten highest mountains.

• See page 10 WORLD'S 10 HIGHEST MOUNTAIN PEAKS.

PHYSICAL MAP OF ASIA

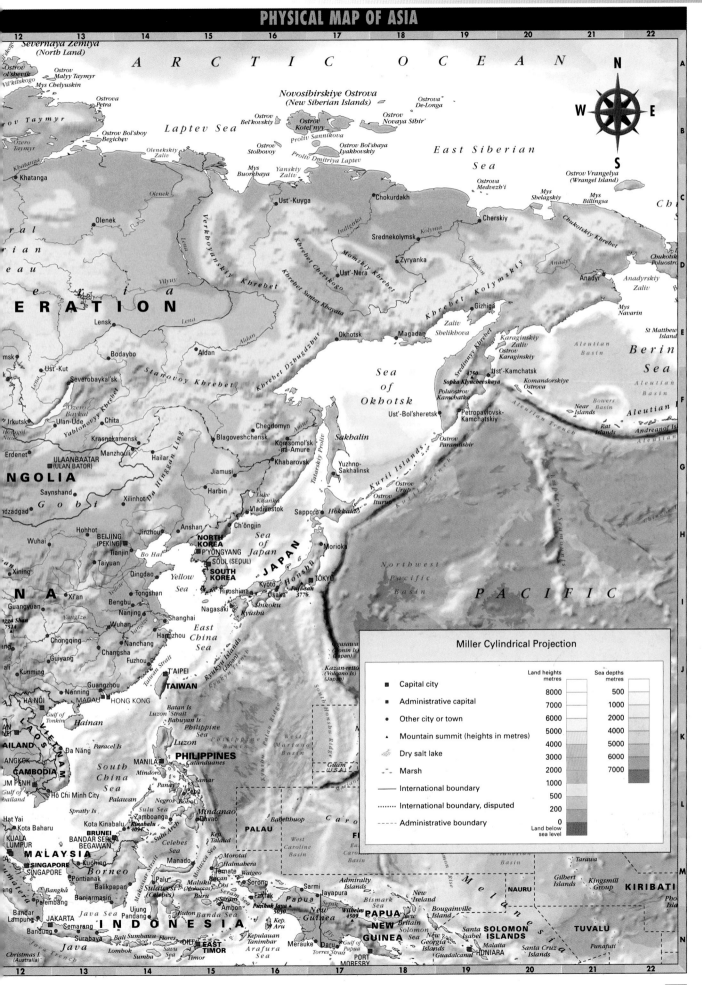

ARCTIC OCEAN

Severnaya Zemlya (North Land)
Ostrov ol'shevik
Vil'kitskogo
Ostrov Malyy Taymyr
Mys Chelyuskin
Ostrova Petra
ov Taymyr
Ostrov Bol'shoy Begichev
Ozero Taymyr
Khatanga
Khatanga
Olenek
Olenek
Olenekskiy Zaliv

Laptev Sea

Novosibirskiye Ostrova (New Siberian Islands)
Ostrov Kotel'nyy
Proliv Sannikova
Ostrov Bel'kovskiy
Ostrov Stolbovoy
Mys Buorkhaya
Yanskiy Zaliv
Proliv Dmitriya Laptev
Ostrov Bol'shaya Lyakhovskiy

Ostrova De-Longa
Ostrov Novaya Sibir'

East Siberian Sea

Ostrova Medvezh'i
Ostrov Vrangelya (Wrangel Island)
Mys Shelagskiy
Mys Billingsa
Ch
S

Ust'-Kuyga
Chokurdakh
Indigirka
Cherskiy
Chukotskiy Khrebet
Anadyrskiy Zaliv

Srednekolymsk
Kolyma
Zyryanka
Momskiy Khrebet
Ust'-Nera
Anadyr
Mys Navarin

ERATION

Lensk
Vilyuy
Lena
r i a
Verkhoyanskiy Khrebet
Khrebet Chersk ogo
Khrebet Suntar Khayata
Kolyma
Gizhiga
Khrebet Kolymskiy

St Matthew Island

Olenek
Bodaybo
Aldan
Aldan
Stanovoy Khrebet
Khrebet Dzhugdzhur
Okhotsk
Zaliv Shelikhova
Magadan
Karaginskiy Zaliv
Sredinnyy Khrebet
Ostrov Karaginskiy
Aleutian Basin
Berin
Sea

msk
Ust'-Kut
Severobaykal'sk
Ozero Baykal
Irkutsk
Ulan-Ude
Yablonovyy Khrebet
Chita
Krasnokamensk

Sea of Okhotsk
Ust'-Bol'sheretsk
4750 Sopka Klyuchevskaya
Poluostrov Kamchatka
Petropavlovsk-Kamchatskiy
Komandorskiye Ostrova
Near Islands
Bowers Basin
Aleutian Basin
Aleutian Trench
Rat Islands
Andreanof Is
Aleutian

Erdenet
ULAANBAATAR (ULAN BATOR)
Manzhouli
Hailar
Da Hinggan Ling
Chegdomyn
Amur
Blagoveshchensk
Komsomol'sk -na-Amure
Khabarovsk
Tatarskiy Proliv
Sakhalin
Ostrov Paramushir
Kuril Trench

NGOLIA
Saynshand
Xilinhot
Jiamusi
Harbin
Lake Khanka
Ostrov Urup
Ostrov Iturup
Kuril Islands

idzadgad
G o b i
Hohhot
Wuhai
Xining
BEIJING (PEKING)
Jinzhou
Anshan
Ch'ŏngjin
Vladivostok
Sapporo
Hokkaidō

NA
Xi'an
Taiyuan
Tianjin
Bo Hai
NORTH KOREA
P'YONGYANG
SOUL (SEOUL)
SOUTH KOREA
Sea of Japan
Morioka
Northwest Pacific Basin

Guangyuan
Yellow Sea
Qingdao
Kyōto
Osaka
JAPAN
Honshū
Fuji-San 3776
TŌKYŌ

Bengbu
Nanjing
Tongshan
Hiroshima
Nagasaki
Shikoku
Kyūshū
PACIFIC

Chongqing
Yangtze
Wuhan
Shanghai
Hangzhou
East China Sea
gge Shan 7514

Guiyang
Changsha
Nanchang
Fuzhou
Ryukyu Islands
Ryukyu Trench

Kunming
Guiyang
T'AIPEI
TAIWAN
Taiwan Strait

HA NOI
Nanning
Guangzhou
MACAU
HONG KONG
Batan Is
Luzon Strait
Babuyan Is
Philippine Sea
West Mariana Basin
Kyushu Palau Ridge

AILAND
Hainan
Gulf of Tonkin
Paracel Is
Luzon

ANGKOK
Đa Năng
South China Sea
MANILA
PHILIPPINES
Calanduanes

CAMBODIA
JM PENH
Gulf of Thailand
Hồ Chi Minh City
Spratly Is
Mindoro
Samar
Panay
Cebu
Guam (USA)

Hat Yai
Kota Baharu
Kota Kinabalu
Palawan
Negros
Bohol
PALAU
Babelthuop
West Caroline Basin
Caro
Mindanao
Davao

KUALA LUMPUR
BRUNEI
BANDAR SERI BEGAWAN
Kinabalu 4094
Zamboanga
Sulu Sea
Sulu Arch

MALAYSIA
SINGAPORE
SINGAPORE
Kuching
Celebes Sea
Manado
Morotai
Halmahera
West Caroline Basin

Bangka
Pontianak
Balikpapan
Borneo
Ternate
Waigeo
Sorong
Admiralty Islands
Bismarck Sea
NAURU
Tarawa
Gilbert Islands
Kingsmill Group
KIRIBATI

Palembang
Banjarmasin
Makassar Strait
Palu
Sulawesi (Celebes)
Maluku (Moluccas)
Buru
Seram
Ambon
Sarmi
Jayapura
Sepik
New Ireland
Bougainville Island
Melanesia

Bandar Lampung
JAKARTA
Semarang
Surabaya
Ujung Pandang
Buton
Banda Sea
Kep. Aru
Puncak Jaya 5030
Papua
Wilhelm 4509
PAPUA NEW GUINEA
New Britain
Solomon Sea
New Georgia Islands
SOLOMON ISLANDS
Santa Isabel
Malaita
HONIARA
Guadalcanal
Santa Cruz Islands
TUVALU

Bandung
INDONESIA
Bali
Sumbawa
Flores
DILI
EAST TIMOR
Timor
Kepulauan Tanimbar
Merauke
Daru
Gulf of Papua
PORT MORESBY
Funafuti

Christmas I. (Australia)
Java
Lombok
Sumba
Savu
Timor
Arafura Sea
Torres Strait
Java Trench

Miller Cylindrical Projection

■ Capital city
■ Administrative capital
● Other city or town
▲ Mountain summit (heights in metres)
Dry salt lake
Marsh
— International boundary
······· International boundary, disputed
---- Administrative boundary

Land heights metres	Sea depths metres
8000	500
7000	1000
6000	2000
5000	4000
4000	5000
3000	6000
2000	7000
1000	
500	
200	
0	
Land below sea level	

HABITATS: ASIA

This map shows the different types of habitat across the continent.

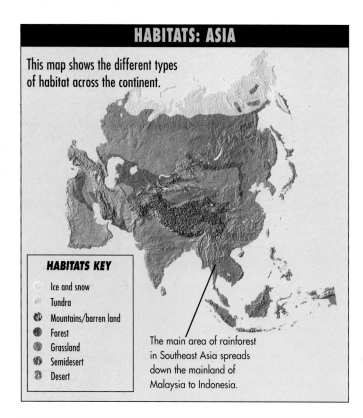

HABITATS KEY

- Ice and snow
- Tundra
- Mountains/barren land
- Forest
- Grassland
- Semidesert
- Desert

The main area of rainforest in Southeast Asia spreads down the mainland of Malaysia to Indonesia.

THE ASIAN RAINFOREST

In just one 10-hectare plot of Malaysian rainforest, scientists found 780 different species of trees. However, Asian rainforests are being destroyed fast.

In the Malaysian rainforest around 25% of bird species and 50% of mammal species, including the orang-utan, will become extinct by 2020 if deforestation continues.

There are only 20,000 orang-utans left living in the wild. They live in Sumatra and Borneo.

In the Tanjung Puting Park in Borneo 6,000 orang-utans live in a protected zone, along with 220 species of birds, 600 species of trees and 200 species of orchid.

- *See page 24 AMAZON RAINFOREST FACTS.*
- *See page 32 PROTECTING AFRICA'S RAINFOREST.*

LAND USE

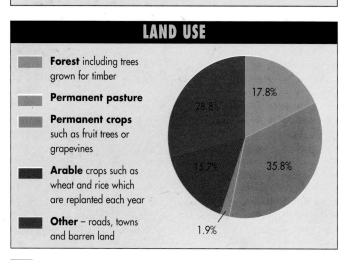

- **Forest** including trees grown for timber
- **Permanent pasture**
- **Permanent crops** such as fruit trees or grapevines
- **Arable** crops such as wheat and rice which are replanted each year
- **Other** – roads, towns and barren land

17.8%
28.8%
15.7%
35.8%
1.9%

CLIMATE: ASIA

TEMPERATURES IN JANUARY

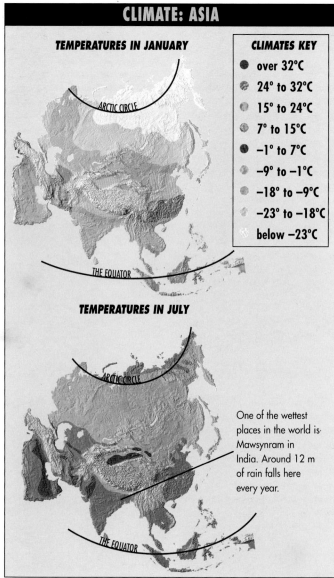

CLIMATES KEY

- over 32°C
- 24° to 32°C
- 15° to 24°C
- 7° to 15°C
- −1° to 7°C
- −9° to −1°C
- −18° to −9°C
- −23° to −18°C
- below −23°C

ARCTIC CIRCLE

THE EQUATOR

TEMPERATURES IN JULY

ARCTIC CIRCLE

THE EQUATOR

One of the wettest places in the world is Mawsynram in India. Around 12 m of rain falls here every year.

FAST FACTS

- Indonesia is the greatest archipelago, or chain of islands, in the world. It stretches for 5,600 m from the Indian Ocean to the Pacific Ocean and is made up of 13,000 islands, with around 400 volcanoes, 100 of which are active.

- The world's most spoken language is Chinese – 13.69% of the world's people speak Chinese as their main language.

- The Maldives island group is made up of 1,196 coral islands. Only 203 are inhabited and the average height above sea level of the islands is just 1.8 m.

- The Dead Sea is a landlocked salt lake between Israel and Jordan. The Dead Sea is 408 m below sea level and is the lowest body of water on Earth.

- Hong Kong is made up of over 200 small islands.

Skyscrapers in Hong Kong.

ASIA FACTFILES

Each country by country factfile contains: **total area** of the country in square kilometres; **total population**; name of the **capital city**; the main **currency** used in the country; **main languages spoken** (listed in order of number of speakers); **top five farming products produced** (listed in order of importance to the country's economy); **natural resources** (of commercial importance); and a country's **status** if it is not independent.

AFGHANISTAN
Total area (sq km): 647,500
Total population: 29,928,987
Capital city: Kabul
Currency: Afghani (AFA)
Languages: Afghan Persian or Dari; Pashtu
Farming (top 5 products): Opium; wheat; fruit; nuts; sheep
Natural resources (top 5): Natural gas; oil; coal; copper; chromite

ARMENIA
Total area (sq km): 29,800
Total population: 2,982,904
Capital city: Yerevan
Currency: Dram (AMD)
Languages: Armenian; Yezidi
Farming: Fruit (especially grapes); vegetables; livestock
Natural resources (top 5): Gold; copper; molybdenum; zinc; alumina

AZERBAIJAN
Total area (sq km): 86,600
Total population: 7,911,974
Capital city: Baki
Currency: Azerbaijani manat (AZM)
Languages: Azerbaijani; Russian; Armenian
Farming (top 5 products): Cotton; cereal crops; rice; grapes; fruit
Natural resources: Oil; natural gas; metals (including iron)

BAHRAIN
Total area (sq km): 665
Total population: 453,237
Capital city: Manama
Currency: Bahraini dinar (BHD)
Languages: Arabic; English; Farsi; Urdu
Farming: Fruit; vegetables; poultry; dairy products
Natural resources: Oil; natural gas; fish; pearls

BANGLADESH
Total area (sq km): 144,000
Total population: 144,319,628
Capital city: Dhaka
Currency: Taka (BDT)
Languages: Bangla (or Bengali); English
Farming (top 5 products): Rice; jute; tea; wheat; sugar cane
Natural resources: Natural gas; arable land; timber; coal

BHUTAN
Total area (sq km): 47,000
Total population: 2,232,291
Capital city: Thimphu
Currency: Ngultrum (BTN); Indian rupee (INR)
Languages: Dzongkha; Tibetan and Nepalese dialects
Farming (top 5 products): Rice; corn; vegetables; citrus fruits; cereal crops
Natural resources: Timber; hydroelectric power; gypsum; calcium carbonate

BRUNEI
Total area (sq km): 5,770
Total population: 372,361
Capital city: Bandar Seri Begawan
Currency: Bruneian dollar (BND)
Languages: Malay; English; Chinese
Farming (top 5 products): Rice; vegetables; fruit; poultry; water buffalo
Natural resources: Oil; natural gas; timber

CAMBODIA
Total area (sq km): 181,040
Total population: 13,607,069
Capital city: Phnom Penh
Currency: Riel (KHR)
Languages: Khmer; French; English
Farming (top 5 products): Rice; rubber; corn; vegetables; cashew nuts
Natural resources (top 5): Oil; natural gas; timber; gemstones; iron ore

CHINA
Total area (sq km): 9,596,960
Total population: 1,306,313,812
Capital city: Beijing
Currency: Yuan (CNY)
Languages: Mandarin Chinese
Farming (top 5 products): Rice; wheat; potatoes; corn; peanuts
Natural resources (top 5): Coal; iron ore; oil; natural gas; mercury

EAST TIMOR
Total area (sq km): 15,007
Total population: 1,040,880
Capital city: Dili
Currency: US dollar (USD)
Languages: Tetum; Portuguese; Indonesian; English
Farming (top 5 products): Coffee; rice; maize; cassava; sweet potatoes
Natural resources (top 5): Gold; oil; natural gas; manganese; marble

GAZA STRIP
Total area (sq km): 360
Total population: 1,376,289
Capital city: Gaza
Currency: New Israeli shekel (ILS)
Languages: Arabic
Farming (top 5 products): Olives; citrus fruits; vegetables; cattle; dairy products
Natural resources: Arable land; natural gas
Status: Semi-autonomous region

GEORGIA
Total area (sq km): 69,700
Total population: 4,677,401
Capital city: T'bilisi
Currency: Lari (GEL)
Languages: Georgian; Russian; Armenian
Farming (top 5 products): Citrus fruits; grapes; tea; hazelnuts; vegetables
Natural resources (top 5): Timber; hydroelectric power; manganese; iron ore; copper

HONG KONG
Total area (sq km): 1,092
Total population: 6,898,686
Capital city: Hong Kong
Currency: Hong Kong dollar (HKD)
Languages: Chinese; English
Farming: Vegetables; poultry
Natural resources: Deepwater harbour; feldspar
Status: Semi-autonomous territory of China

INDIA
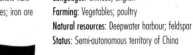
Total area (sq km): 3,287,590
Total population: 1,080,264,388
Capital city: New Delhi
Currency: Indian rupee (INR)
Languages: English; Hindi; Bengali; Telugu; Marathi; Tamil; Urdu; Gujarati
Farming (top 5 products): Rice; wheat; oilseed; cotton; jute
Natural resources (top 5): Coal; iron ore; manganese; mica; bauxite

INDONESIA

Total area (sq km): 1,919,440
Total population: 241,973,879
Capital city: Jakarta
Currency: Indonesian rupiah (IDR)
Languages: Bahasa Indonesia; English; Dutch; Javanese
Farming (top 5 products): Rice; cassava; peanuts; rubber; cocoa
Natural resources (top 5): Oil; tin; natural gas; nickel; timber

IRAN

Total area (sq km): 1,648,000
Total population: 68,017,860
Capital city: Tehran
Currency: Iranian rial (IRR)
Languages: Persian; Turkic; Kurdish
Farming (top 5 products): Wheat; rice; cereal crops; sugar beets; fruit
Natural resources (top 5): Oil; natural gas; coal; chromium; copper

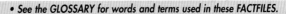
• See the GLOSSARY for words and terms used in these FACTFILES.

ASIA *Factfiles*

IRAQ

Total area (sq km): 437,072
Total population: 26,074,906
Capital city: Baghdad
Currency: New Iraqi dinar (NID)
Languages: Arabic; Kurdish; Assyrian; Armenian
Farming (top 5 products): Wheat; barley; rice; vegetables; dates
Natural resources (top 5): Oil; natural gas; phosphates; sulphur

ISRAEL
Total area (sq km): 20,770
Total population: 6,276,883
Capital city: Jerusalem
Currency: New Israeli shekel (ILS)
Languages: Hebrew; Arabic; English
Farming (top 5 products): Citrus fruits; vegetables;
cotton; cattle; poultry
Natural resources (top 5): Timber; potash; copper;
natural gas; phosphate

JAPAN
Total area (sq km): 377,835
Total population: 127,417,244
Capital city: Tokyo
Currency: Yen (JPY)
Languages: Japanese
Farming (top 5 products): Rice; sugar beets; vegetables; fruit; pigs
Natural resources: Fish

JORDAN
Total area (sq km): 92,300
Total population: 5,759,732
Capital city: 'Amman
Currency: Jordanian dinar (JOD)
Languages: Arabic; English
Farming (top 5 products): Wheat; barley; citrus fruits;
tomatoes; melons
Natural resources: Phosphates; potash; oil shale

KAZAKHSTAN
Total area (sq km): 2,717,300
Total population: 15,185,844
Capital city: Astana
Currency: Tenge (KZT)
Languages: Kazakh; Russian
Farming: Cereal crops; cotton; livestock
Natural resources (top 5): Oil; natural gas; coal; iron ore; manganese

KUWAIT
Total area (sq km): 17,820
Total population: 1,044,294
Capital city: Kuwait
Currency: Kuwaiti dinar (KD)
Languages: Arabic; English
Farming: No farming
Natural resources: Oil; fish; shrimp; natural gas

KYRGYZSTAN

Total area (sq km): 198,500
Total population: 5,146,281
Capital city: Bishkek
Currency: Kyrgyz som (KGS)
Languages: Kyrgyz; Russian
Farming (top 5 products): Tobacco; cotton; potatoes; vegetables; grapes
Natural resources (top 5): Hydroelectric power; gold; coal; oil;
natural gas

LAOS

Total area (sq km): 236,800
Total population: 6,217,141
Capital city: Vientiane
Currency: Kip (LAK)
Languages: Lao; French; English
Farming (top 5 products): Sweet potatoes; vegetables; corn; coffee;
sugar cane
Natural resources (top 5): Timber; hydroelectric power;
gypsum; tin; gold

LEBANON

Total area (sq km): 10,400
Total population: 3,826,018
Capital city: Beirut
Currency: Lebanese pound (LBP)
Languages: Arabic; French; English; Armenian
Farming (top 5 products): Citrus fruits; grapes; tomatoes; apples;
vegetables
Natural resources: Limestone; iron ore; salt;
surplus water (in an area where water is scarce)

MACAU
Total area (sq km): 25.4
Total population: 449,198
Capital city: Macau
Currency: Pataca (MOP)
Languages: Chinese (Cantonese)
Farming: Limited farming
Natural resources: Fish; shellfish
Status: Semi-autonomous territory of China

MALAYSIA

Total area (sq km): 329,750
Total population: 23,953,136
Capital city: Kuala Lumpur
Currency: Ringgit (MYR)
Languages: Bahasa Melayu; English; Chinese dialects; Tamil
Farming (top 5 products): Rubber; palm oil; cocoa; rice; timber
Natural resources (top 5): Tin; oil; timber; copper; iron ore

MALDIVES
Total area (sq km): 300
Total population: 349,106
Capital city: Male
Currency: Rufiyaa (MVR)
Languages: Maldivian Dhivehi; English spoken by government officials
Farming: Coconuts; corn; sweet potatoes
Natural resources: Fish

MONGOLIA
Total area (sq km): 1,564,116
Total population: 2,791,272
Capital city: Ulaanbaatar
Currency: Tugrik (MNT)
Languages: Khalkha Mongol; Turkic; Russian
Farming (top 5 products): Wheat; barley; vegetables; crops for animal
feed; livestock (including camels and horses)
Natural resources (top 5): Oil; coal; copper; molybdenum; tungsten

MYANMAR (BURMA)

Total area (sq km): 678,500
Total population: 42,909,464
Capital city: Yangon (Rangoon)
Currency: Kyat (MMK)
Languages: Burmese
Farming (top 5 products): Rice; pulses; beans; sesame; groundnuts
Natural resources (top 5): Oil; timber; tin; antimony; zinc

NEPAL
Total area (sq km): 140,800
Total population: 27,676,547
Capital city: Kathmandu
Currency: Nepalese rupee (NPR)
Languages: Nepali; Maithali
Farming (top 5 products): Rice; corn; wheat; sugar cane; vegetables
Natural resources (top 5): Oil; natural gas; fish; salt; limestone

NORTH KOREA

Total area (sq km): 120,540
Total population: 22,912,177
Capital city: Pyongyang
Currency: North Korean won (KPW)
Languages: Korean
Farming (top 5 products): Rice; corn; potatoes; soybeahs; pulses
Natural resources (top 5): Coal; lead; tungsten; zinc; graphite

OMAN
Total area (sq km): 212,460
Total population: 2,424,290
Capital city: Muscat
Currency: Omani rial (OMR)
Languages: Arabic; English; Baluchi; Urdu; Indian dialects
Farming (top 5 products): Dates; limes; bananas; alfalfa; vegetables
Natural resources (top 5): Oil; copper; asbestos; marble; limestone

PAKISTAN

Total area (sq km): 803,940
Total population: 162,419,946
Capital city: Islamabad
Currency: Pakistani rupee (PKR)
Languages: Punjabi; Sindhi; Siraiki; Pashtu; Urdu
Farming (top 5 products): Cotton; wheat; rice; sugar cane; fruit
Natural resources (top 5): Natural gas; oil; coal; iron ore; copper

PHILIPPINES
Total area (sq km): 300,000
Total population: 87,857,473
Capital city: Manila
Currency: Philippine peso (PHP)
Languages: Filipino; English; Tagalog; Cebuano
Farming (top 5 products): Sugar cane; coconuts; rice; corn; bananas
Natural resources (top 5): Timber; oil; nickel; cobalt; silver

QATAR
Total area (sq km): 11,437
Total population: 863,051
Capital city: Doha
Currency: Qatari rial (QAR)
Languages: Arabic; English
Farming (top 5 products): Fruit; vegetables; poultry; dairy products; cattle
Natural resources: Oil; natural gas; fish

SAUDI ARABIA
Total area (sq km): 1,960,582
Total population: 20,841,523
Capital city: Riyadh
Currency: Saudi riyal (SAR)
Languages: Arabic
Farming (top 5 products): Wheat; barley; tomatoes; melons; dates
Natural resources (top 5): Oil; natural gas; iron ore; gold; copper

SINGAPORE
Total area (sq km): 692.7
Total population: 4,425,720
Capital city: Singapore
Currency: Singapore dollar (SGD)
Languages: Chinese (Mandarin); English; Malay
Farming (top 5 products): Rubber; copra; fruit; orchids; vegetables
Natural resources: Fish; deepwater ports (suitable for shipping)

SOUTH KOREA
Total area (sq km): 98,480
Total population: 48,422,644
Capital city: Seoul
Currency: South Korean won (KRW)
Languages: Korean
Farming (top 5 products): Rice; vegetables; barley; fruit; livestock
Natural resources (top 5): Coal; tungsten; graphite; molybdenum; lead

SRI LANKA
Total area (sq km): 65,610
Total population: 20,064,776
Capital city: Sri Jayewardenepura Kotte
Currency: Sri Lankan rupee (LKR)
Languages: Sinhala; Tamil; English
Farming (top 5 products): Rice; sugar cane; cereal crops; pulses; oilseed
Natural resources (top 5): Limestone; graphite; mineral sands; gemstones; phosphates

SYRIA
Total area (sq km): 185,180
Total population: 18,448,752
Capital city: Damascus
Currency: Syrian pound (SYP)
Languages: Arabic; Kurdish
Farming (top 5 products): Wheat; barley; cotton; lentils; chickpeas
Natural resources (top 5): Oil; phosphates; chrome ore; manganese; asphalt

TAIWAN
Total area (sq km): 35,980
Total population: 22,894,384
Capital city: Taipei
Currency: New Taiwan dollar (TWD)
Languages: Chinese (Mandarin); Taiwanese
Farming (top 5 products): Rice; corn; vegetables; fruit; tea
Natural resources (top 5): Coal; natural gas; limestone; marble; asbestos
Status: Self-governing territory of China

TAJIKISTAN
Total area (sq km): 143,100
Total population: 7,163,506
Capital city: Dushanbe
Currency: Somoni
Languages: Tajik; Russian
Farming (top 5 products): Cotton; cereal crops; fruit; grapes; vegetables
Natural resources (top 5): Hydroelectric power; oil; uranium; mercury; coal

THAILAND
Total area (sq km): 514,000
Total population: 65,444,371
Capital city: Bangkok
Currency: Baht (THB)
Languages: Thai; English
Farming (top 5 products): Rice; cassava; rubber; corn; sugar cane
Natural resources (top 5): Tin; rubber; natural gas; tungsten; tantalum

TURKMENISTAN
Total area (sq km): 488,100
Total population: 4,952,081
Capital city: Ashgabat
Currency: Turkmen manat (TMM)
Languages: Turkmen; Russian; Uzbek
Farming: Cotton; cereal crops; livestock
Natural resources: Oil; natural gas; sulphur; salt

UNITED ARAB EMIRATES
Total area (sq km): 82,880
Total population: 957,133
Capital city: Abu Dhabi
Currency: Emirati dirham (AED)
Languages: Arabic; Persian; English; Hindi; Urdu
Farming (top 5 products): Dates; vegetables; water melons; poultry; eggs
Natural resources: Oil; natural gas

UZBEKISTAN
Total area (sq km): 447,400
Total population: 26,851,195
Capital city: Toshkent
Currency: Uzbekistani sum (UZS)
Languages: Uzbek; Russian; Tajik
Farming (top 5 products): Cotton; vegetables; fruit; cereal crops; livestock
Natural resources (top 5): Natural gas; oil; coal; gold; uranium

VIETNAM
Total area (sq km): 329,560
Total population: 83,535,576
Capital city: Hanoi
Currency: Dong (VND)
Languages: Vietnamese; English; French; Chinese; Khmer
Farming (top 5 products): Rice; coffee; rubber; cotton; tea
Natural resources (top 5): Phosphates; coal; manganese; bauxite; chromate

WEST BANK
Total area (sq km): 5,860
Total population: 2,385,615
Capital city: West Bank
Currency: New Israeli shekel (ILS); Jordanian dinar (JOD)
Languages: Arabic; Hebrew; English
Farming (top 5 products): Olives; citrus fruits; vegetables; cattle; dairy products
Natural resources: Arable land
Status: Disputed territory

YEMEN
Total area (sq km): 527,970
Total population: 20,727,063
Capital city: Sanaa
Currency: Yemeni rial (YER)
Languages: Arabic
Farming (top 5 products): Cereal crops; fruit; vegetables; pulses; qat (a mildly narcotic shrub)
Natural resources (top 5): Oil; fish; rock salt; marble; coal

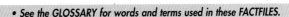

• See the GLOSSARY for words and terms used in these FACTFILES.

Tigers are the largest member of the cat family. They live in a variety of habitats in southeast Asia – from hot jungle regions, in countries such as India, to the cold coniferous forests of Siberia.

• See page 55
OCEANIA FACTFILES.

In this book the term Oceania refers to the countries of Australia, New Zealand and Papua New Guinea, and the islands of the South Pacific. Oceania stretches across a vast area of ocean and includes 20,000 or so islands which make up the regions of Micronesia, Melanesia and Polynesia. Thousands of the islands are uninhabited, and many are formed from coral reefs and underwater volcanoes. Papua New Guinea is made up of the eastern half of the island of New Guinea and around 600 smaller islands.

The Great Barrier Reef is a complex of coral reefs, sandbanks and small islands off the northeastern coast of Australia.

FAST FACTS

• The Great Barrier Reef spreads for over 2,000 km along Australia's coast. It covers an area of 350,000 sq km.

• The capital of New Zealand, Wellington, is the most southerly capital city in the world.

• Australia has a total of 1,371,000 sq km of desert — 16% of Australia is desert land.

• The Kwajalein atoll, in the Marshall Islands, is a ring of coral enclosing a lagoon of around 2,850 sq km. It is the biggest atoll in the world.

• The Marshall islands comprise two island chains which include 30 atolls and 1,152 islands.

• The 5.5 million people of Papua New Guinea speak around 800 different languages.

• New Zealand uses hydroelectric power and has very little industry so it is one of the cleanest, least-polluted countries in the world.

HIGHEST MOUNTAINS (BY COUNTRY)

NAME	LOCATION	HEIGHT (metres)
Mt Wilhelm	Papua New Guinea	4,509
Mt Cook	New Zealand	3,754
Mt Kosciuszko	Australia	2,230

LARGEST ISLANDS

NAME		AREA (sq km)
New Guinea Island (total area of island including Indonesian section)		821,000
South Island	New Zealand	150,499
North Island	New Zealand	114,700
Tasmania	Australia	67,800

* Australia is too large to be an island. It is a continental landmass.

HABITATS: OCEANIA

This map shows the different types of habitat across the continent.

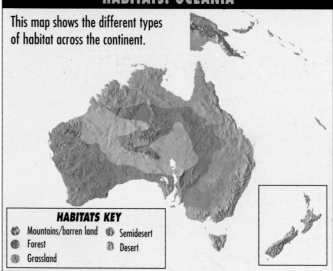

HABITATS KEY
- Mountains/barren land
- Forest
- Grassland
- Semidesert
- Desert

POLITICAL MAP OF OCEANIA

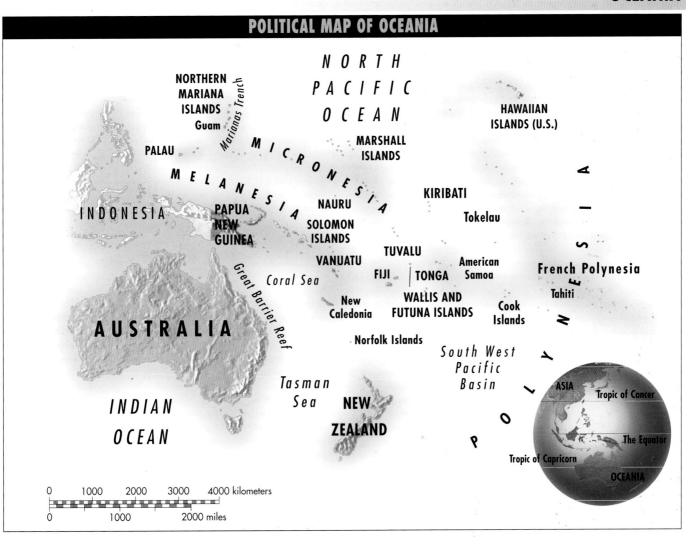

NORTH PACIFIC OCEAN

NORTHERN MARIANA ISLANDS
Guam
Marianas Trench

MICRONESIA

MARSHALL ISLANDS

HAWAIIAN ISLANDS (U.S.)

PALAU

MELANESIA

INDONESIA

PAPUA NEW GUINEA

NAURU

SOLOMON ISLANDS

KIRIBATI

Tokelau

VANUATU

TUVALU

FIJI · TONGA

American Samoa

French Polynesia

Tahiti

Coral Sea

New Caledonia

WALLIS AND FUTUNA ISLANDS

Cook Islands

P O L Y N E S I A

Great Barrier Reef

AUSTRALIA

Norfolk Islands

South West Pacific Basin

INDIAN OCEAN

Tasman Sea

NEW ZEALAND

ASIA
Tropic of Cancer
The Equator
Tropic of Capricorn
OCEANIA

0   1000   2000   3000   4000 kilometers

0   1000   2000 miles

ULURU

Uluru in the desert of central Australia is sacred to the Australian aboriginal people. This oval-shaped, giant block of sandstone is at least 450 million years old. Uluru is 3.5 km long and 2.4 km wide.

LAND USE

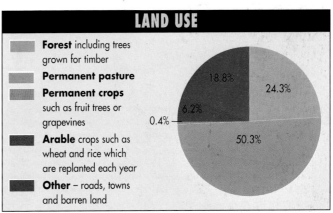

Forest including trees grown for timber

Permanent pasture

Permanent crops such as fruit trees or grapevines

Arable crops such as wheat and rice which are replanted each year

Other – roads, towns and barren land

18.8%
24.3%
0.4%
6.2%
50.3%

CLIMATE: OCEANIA

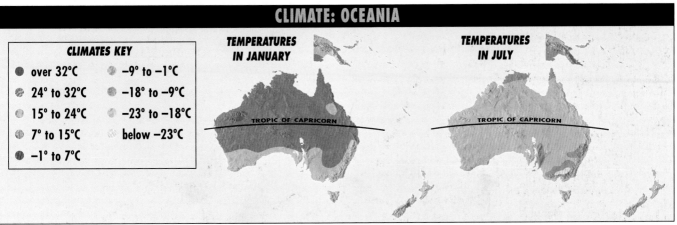

CLIMATES KEY

- over 32°C
- 24° to 32°C
- 15° to 24°C
- 7° to 15°C
- −1° to 7°C
- −9° to −1°C
- −18° to −9°C
- −23° to −18°C
- below −23°C

TEMPERATURES IN JANUARY

TEMPERATURES IN JULY

TROPIC OF CAPRICORN

TROPIC OF CAPRICORN

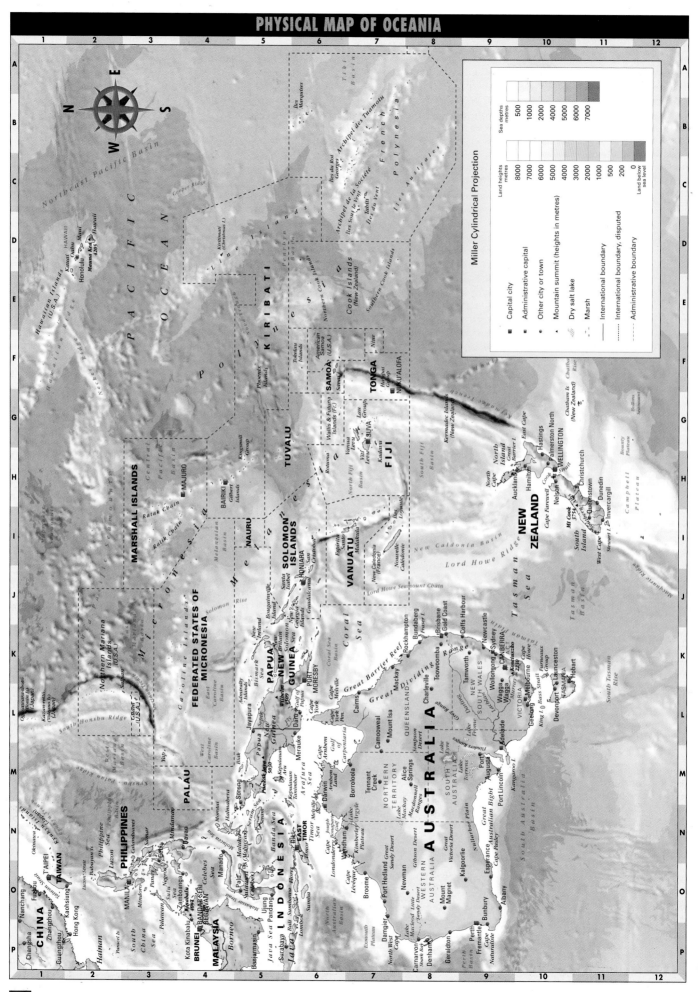

Miller Cylindrical Projection

Sea depths metres
500 · 1000 · 2000 · 4000 · 5000 · 6000 · 7000

Land heights metres
8000 · 7000 · 6000 · 5000 · 4000 · 3000 · 2000 · 1000 · 500 · 200 · 0 Land below sea level

- ■ Capital city
- ■ Administrative capital
- • Other city or town
- ▲ Mountain summit (heights in metres)
- Dry salt lake
- Marsh
- —— International boundary
- ········ International boundary, disputed
- ------ Administrative boundary

OCEANIA FACTFILES

Each country by country factfile contains: **total area** of the country in square kilometres**; total population;** name of the **capital city**; the main **currency** used in the country; **main languages spoken** (listed in order of number of speakers); **top five farming products produced** (listed in order of importance to the country's economy); **natural resources** (of commercial importance); and a country's **status** if it is not independent.

AMERICAN SAMOA

Total area (sq km): 199
Total population: 57,881
Capital city: Pago Pago
Currency: US dollar (USD)
Languages: Samoan; English
Farming: Bananas; coconuts; vegetables; taro
Natural resources: Pumice
Status: United States unincorporated territory

AUSTRALIA
Total area (sq km): 7,686,850
Total population: 20,090,437
Capital city: Canberra
Currency: Australian dollar (AUD)
Languages: English
Farming (top 5 products): Wheat; barley; sugar cane; fruit; livestock
Natural resources (top 5): Bauxite; coal; iron ore; copper; tin

COOK ISLANDS
Total area (sq km): 240
Total population: 21,388
Capital city: Avarua
Currency: New Zealand dollar (NZD)
Languages: English; Maori
Farming (top 5 products): Copra; citrus fruits; pineapples; tomatoes; beans
Natural resources: No natural resources
Status: New Zealand overseas territory

FIJI
Total area (sq km): 18,270
Total population: 893,354
Capital city: Suva
Currency: Fijian dollar (FJD)
Languages: English; Fijian; Hindustani
Farming (top 5 products): Sugar cane; coconuts; cassava; rice; sweet potatoes
Natural resources (top 5): Timber; fish; gold; copper; oil potential

FRENCH POLYNESIA
Total area (sq km): 4,167
Total population: 270,485
Capital city: Papeete
Currency: Comptoirs Francais du Pacifique franc (XPF)
Languages: French; Polynesian
Farming (top 5 products): Coconuts; vanilla; vegetables; fruit; poultry
Natural resources: Timber; fish; cobalt; hydroelectric power
Status: French overseas territory

GUAM
Total area (sq km): 549
Total population: 168,564
Capital city: Hagatna
Currency: US dollar (USD)
Languages: English; Chamorro; Philippine languages
Farming (top 5 products): Fruit; copra; vegetables; eggs; livestock
Natural resources: Fish
Status: United States unincorporated territory

KIRIBATI
Total area (sq km): 811
Total population: 103,092
Capital city: Tarawa
Currency: Australian dollar (AUD)
Languages: I-Kiribati; English
Farming: Copra; taro; breadfruit; vegetables
Natural resources: No natural resources

MARSHALL ISLANDS
Total area (sq km): 181.3
Total population: 59,071
Capital city: Majuro
Currency: US dollar (USD)
Languages: Marshallese; English
Farming (top 5 products): Coconuts; tomatoes; melons; taro; breadfruit
Natural resources: Coconuts; fish; deep seabed minerals

MICRONESIA (FEDERATED STATES OF)
Total area (sq km): 702
Total population: 108,105
Capital city: Palikir
Currency: US dollar (USD)
Languages: English; Trukese; Pohnpeian; Yapese; Kosrean; Ulithian
Farming (top 5 products): Black pepper; tropical fruit and vegetables; coconuts; cassava; betel nuts
Natural resources: Timber; fish; deep seabed minerals; phosphate

NAURU
Total area (sq km): 21
Total population: 13,048
Capital city: No capital – government offices in Yaren district
Currency: Australian dollar (AUD)
Languages: Nauruan; English
Farming: Coconuts
Natural resources: Phosphates; fish

NEW CALEDONIA
Total area (sq km): 19,060
Total population: 216,494
Capital city: Noumea
Currency: Comptoirs Francais du Pacifique franc (XPF)
Languages: French; 33 Melanesian–Polynesian dialects
Farming: Vegetables; livestock (including deer)
Natural resources (top 5): Nickel; chrome; iron; cobalt; manganese
Status: French overseas territory

NEW ZEALAND
Total area (sq km): 268,680
Total population: 4,035,461
Capital city: Wellington
Currency: New Zealand dollar (NZD)
Languages: English; Maori
Farming (top 5 products): Wheat; barley; potatoes; pulses; fruit
Natural resources (top 5): Natural gas; iron ore; sand; coal; timber

NORTHERN MARIANA ISLANDS
Total area (sq km): 477
Total population: 80,362
Capital city: Saipan
Currency: US dollar (USD)
Languages: Philippine languages; Chinese; Chamorro; English
Farming: Coconuts; fruit; vegetables; cattle
Natural resources: Arable land; fish
Status: United States commonwealth

PALAU
Total area (sq km): 458
Total population: 20,303
Capital city: Koror
Currency: US dollar (USD)
Languages: Palauan; English; Tobi; Angaur
Farming: Coconuts; copra; cassava; sweet potatoes
Natural resources: Timber; gold; fish; deep seabed minerals

PAPUA NEW GUINEA

Total area (sq km): 462,840
Total population: 5,545,268
Capital city: Port Moresby
Currency: Kina (PGK)
Languages: Melanesian; up to 800 indigenous languages
Farming (top 5 products): Coffee; cocoa; coconuts; palm kernels; tea
Natural resources (top 5): Gold; copper; silver; natural gas; timber

SAMOA

Total area (sq km): 2,944
Total population: 177,287
Capital city: Apia
Currency: Tala (SAT)
Languages: Samoan; English
Farming (top 5 products): Coconuts; bananas; taro; yams; coffee
Natural resources: Timber; fish; hydroelectric power

SOLOMON ISLANDS

Total area (sq km): 28,450
Total population: 538,032
Capital city: Honiara
Currency: Solomon Islands dollar (SBD)
Languages: Melanesian; English; 120 indigenous languages
Farming (top 5 products): Cocoa; coconuts; palm kernels; rice; potatoes
Natural resources (top 5): Fish; timber; gold; bauxite; phosphates

TONGA
Total area (sq km): 748
Total population: 112,422
Capital city: Nuku'alofa
Currency: Pa'anga (TOP)
Languages: Tongan; English
Farming (top 5 products): Squash; coconuts; copra; bananas; vanilla
Natural resources: Fish

TUVALU
Total area (sq km): 26
Total population: 11,636
Capital city: Funafuti
Currency: Australian dollar (AUD)
Languages: Tuvaluan; English; Samoan; Kiribati (on island of Nui)
Farming: Coconuts
Natural resources: Fish

VANUATU
Total area (sq km): 12,200
Total population: 205,754
Capital city: Port-Vila
Currency: Vatu (VUV)
Languages: English; French; 100 indigenous languages
Farming (top 5 products): Copra; coconuts; cocoa; coffee; taro
Natural resources: Manganese; timber; fish

WALLIS AND FUTUNA ISLANDS
Total area (sq km): 274
Total population: 16,025
Capital city: Mata-Utu
Currency: Comptoirs Francais du Pacifique franc (XPF)
Languages: Wallisian; Futunian; French
Farming (top 5 products): Breadfruit; yams; taro; bananas; livestock
Natural resources: No natural resources
Status: French overseas territory

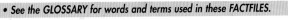
• See the GLOSSARY for words and terms used in these FACTFILES.

Size of Arctic Ocean:
14,056,000 sq km

The Ice Cap:
The Arctic Ocean is surrounded by icy land. A large section of the ocean is permanently frozen. This is called the 'Ice Cap'. In the winter the sea freezes and increases the size of the Ice Cap so that it touches the land.

Arctic temperatures:
Lowest winter temperature −45°C

Arctic seasons:
The sun never rises during the six months of the Arctic winter. In the summer, there are times when the sun never sets.

Arctic animal life:
Polar bears, caribou (reindeer), arctic foxes, seals, whales, narwhals, walruses and sea birds all live in the Arctic.

Polar bear fact:
The polar bear is the only bear with international protection. Scientists estimate there are up to 40,000 polar bears living in the Arctic Circle.

Polar bear hunting grounds:
Polar bears spend the winter and spring on the frozen ocean hunting for harp seals and hooded seals. When the ice thaws for the summer, they move back onto the mainland.

Plant life:
Over 500 different species of flowering plants grow within the Arctic Circle.

Fast fact:
Both the Arctic and Antarctica are classified as 'cold deserts' because most areas receive less than 26 cm of rain or snow each year.

THE ARCTIC

The Arctic region is at the very top of the Earth. The Arctic Circle comprises a shallow, frozen ocean surrounded by the northern edges of Europe, Asia and North America. The area is named after *Arktos*, the Great Bear star constellation, which dominates the northern polar skies. The Arctic circle area is marked on maps with an imaginary line.

Polar bears live in the Arctic Circle. They are the world's largest, land-living predator.

POLITICAL MAP OF THE ARCTIC

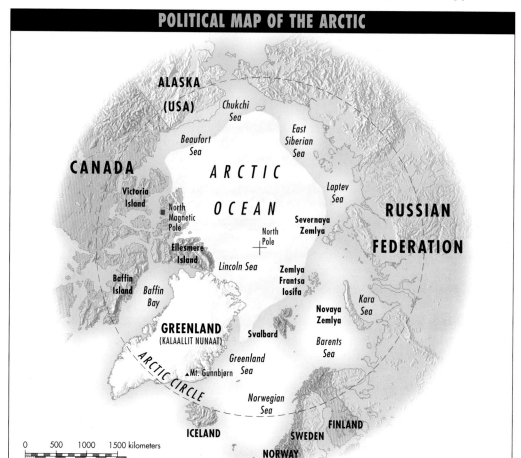

THE ARCTIC ICE

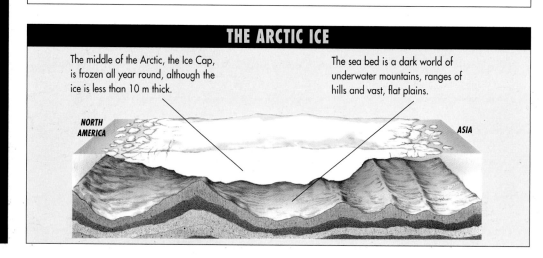

The middle of the Arctic, the Ice Cap, is frozen all year round, although the ice is less than 10 m thick.

The sea bed is a dark world of underwater mountains, ranges of hills and vast, flat plains.

ANTARCTICA

Antarctica is a mountainous continent that is almost completely covered by a gigantic sheet of ice larger than Europe and the USA put together. It is the coldest and windiest place on Earth. Average winter temperatures reach –60°C, and roaring, ferocious winds of up to 290 km/h produce blizzards and snowdrifts.

Emperor Penguins live in the Antarctic. They grow to around one metre tall and are the largest species of Penguin.

ANTARCTICA FACTFILE

SOUTH AMERICA

ANTARCTICA

Antarctic Circle

Antarctica/Arctic:
The name Antarctica means 'opposite the Arctic'. When it is summer in the Arctic it is winter in Antarctica.

Total area of continent:
14,100,000 sq km
98% ice
2% barren rock

Life in Antarctica:
The Antarctic has very little ice-free land even in summer. No land mammals live here. Fewer plants and animals live here than the Arctic. Adelie and Emperor penguins come ashore to breed and lay their eggs here.

Nearest landmass:
South America – the southern tip is approximately 965 km from Antarctica.

Length of coastline:
17,968,000 km

Highest mountain:
Vinson Massif
4,897 m

Lowest point:
Bentley Sub-glacial Trench
–2,555 m below sea level

Population:
No permanent population. Around 1000 to 4000 scientists working at research stations.

Natural resources:
Iron ore, chromium, copper, gold, nickel, platinum and other minerals.

Fast fact:
More than 90% of all the world's fresh water is stored in the ice sheets on Antarctica, and on Greenland (in the Arctic region).

POLITICAL MAP OF ANTARCTICA

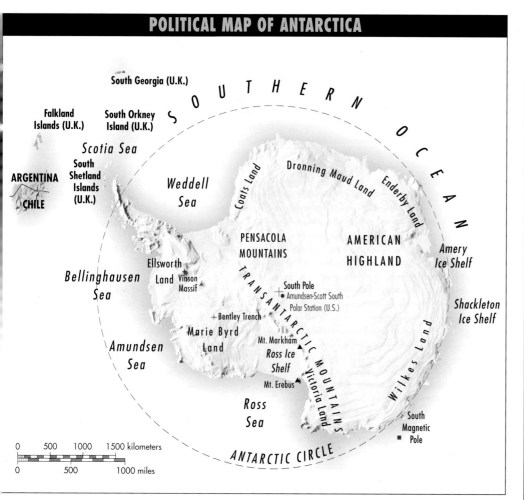

South Georgia (U.K.)

Falkland Islands (U.K.)

South Orkney Island (U.K.)

SOUTHERN OCEAN

Scotia Sea

ARGENTINA

CHILE

South Shetland Islands (U.K.)

Weddell Sea

Coats Land

Dronning Maud Land

Enderby Land

Bellinghausen Sea

PENSACOLA MOUNTAINS

AMERICAN HIGHLAND

Amery Ice Shelf

Ellsworth Land

Vinson Massif

South Pole
Amundsen-Scott South
Polar Station (U.S.)

Shackleton Ice Shelf

TRANSANTARCTIC MOUNTAINS

Bentley Trench

Marie Byrd Land

Wilkes Land

Amundsen Sea

Mt. Markham

Ross Ice Shelf

Mt. Erebus

Victoria Land

Ross Sea

South Magnetic Pole

ANTARCTIC CIRCLE

0	500	1000	1500 kilometers

0	500	1000 miles

THE ANTARCTIC ICE

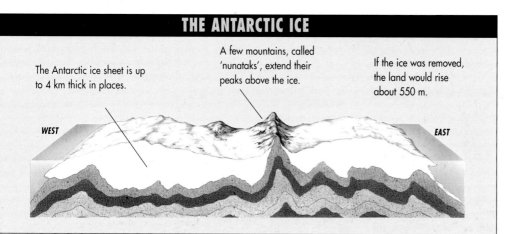

The Antarctic ice sheet is up to 4 km thick in places.

A few mountains, called 'nunataks', extend their peaks above the ice.

If the ice was removed, the land would rise about 550 m.

WEST

EAST

GLOSSARY

Afrikaans A language of South Africa, closely related to Dutch.

Amerindian A word used to describe Native Americans, or American Indians. When Christopher Columbus reached the Americas he thought he had reached Asia and the East Indies, which is why the word Indian first came to be used in connection with people living in America.

Arable land Land which is suitable for growing crops.

Aragonite A mineral consisting of calcium carbonate. It can be found in white sea shells and as deposits in hot springs (naturally hot water heated by underground volcanic activity).

Archipelago A group of islands, or an area of sea containing many islands.

Atoll A ring-shaped reef, island or chain of islands formed from coral.

Bantu A 'language family' used by over 400 different ethnic groups in Africa, from Cameroon to South Africa.

Bauxite The ore from which aluminium is extracted.

Berber A people belonging to northwest Africa, chiefly living in Morocco and Algeria, although some now live in Egypt and as far south as Burkina Faso.

Borders Lines separating geographical or political areas, especially the edges of countries. Borders are normally drawn up by governments. Borders can change over time as countries take over new territory, join with other countries or split into smaller countries.

Calcium carbonate An insoluble, white solid which can be found in marble, chalk, limestone and calcite, and in sea shells and some corals. It is used to make cement.

Cassava The starchy, tuber-like root of a tropical tree. It is used as food, and is sometimes called manioc.

Chain (of mountains) A line of mountains made up of more than one mountain range.

Chicle A milky, latex liquid obtained from the sapodilla tree. It is used to make chewing gum.

Climate The average temperature and weather conditions in a particular region over a period of years.

Continent One of the Earth's large, continuous landmasses: Africa, Antarctica, Asia, Australia, Europe, North America and South America.

Copra The oil-yielding kernel of the coconut.

Coral The hard, stony substance secreted by marine animals called polyps as an external skeleton.

Coral reef An underwater structure made from coral – the hard, external skeletons of marine animals called polyps. When a polyp dies, its skeleton remains as part of the reef so the reef gradually builds up.

Creole A language formed from the mixing of a local language and a European language, such as French.

Desert A barren area of land with very little, or no rainfall. Deserts are normally sandy or rocky with limited plant and animal life. Deserts can be hot or cold.

Equator An imaginary line around the centre of the Earth. The equator is exactly halfway between the North and South Poles, the most northern and southern points on the Earth, and the axis points the Earth spins on. The Equator divides the Earth into the northern and southern hemispheres (halves).

Faults Cracks in the Earth's crust. The movement of the Earth's tectonic plates causes rocks to move and stretch until the pressure becomes so great that they crack.

Geothermal power Power created for use in homes or industry using the Earth's internal heat. In Iceland the steam from seawater boiled by molten lava, 2 km below the ground, is used by power stations to heat fresh water for homes, and to power turbines to produce electricity.

Gorge A valley with steep, rocky sides between hills or mountains. Gorges are formed over a long time by a river cutting down into the land it flows across.

Graphite A grey form of carbon which occurs in some rocks. Graphite has many uses including as the writing part of pencils.

Hydroelectric power The generation of electricity for use in homes and industry using flowing water. The water is used to drive turbines to power generators.

Indigenous Originating or occurring naturally within a country or a region. It can refer to people, plants or animals.

Infant mortality rate The number of deaths of infants under one year old in a year. It is a measure of the quality of life in a country, including health and wealth.

Kaolin A fine, soft white clay used in the production of china and porcelain, and in some medicines.

Lava Hot, molten (melted) rock expelled from a volcano. When the lava is still inside the Earth it is called magma.

Life expectancy The average number of years a person can be expected to live in a given place. It is a measure of the quality of life in a country, including health and wealth.

Lignite A type of soft, brown coal.

Longitude Lines on a map which run north to south and measure how many degrees east or west a place is from the *Prime Meridian Line* (the imaginary line that runs north to south through Greenwich in London, UK, the place which has been designated *zero degrees longitude*).

Magma Hot, molten (melted) rock inside the Earth's mantle. Magma sometimes escapes onto the Earth's surface through a volcano or other crack in the Earth's crust. As soon as it leaves the Earth, magma is called lava.

Manganese A metallic element, mined and used in the making of steel, pesticides, fertilisers, batteries and some ceramics. It is a hazardous substance and high levels of manganese will attack the nervous system.

Mantle The layer inside the Earth between the Earth's rocky crust and the core. The mantle is made up of soft, molten (melted) rock.

Mayan A 'language family' that includes many American Indian languages spoken by people in Central America.

Molybdenum A brittle, silver-grey metal used in making some kinds of steel.

Nahua A language spoken by indigenous peoples from southern Mexico to Central America. The language dates back to the Aztecs.

Oil shale Fine-grained, sedimentary rock from which oil can be extracted. Sedimentary rock is formed from particles of mud, sand and other debris that have settled and been squashed down to form hard rock.

Ore Rock that contains a metal which can be extracted.

Papiamento A Spanish Creole language which is mixed with portuguese, Dutch and English. It is spoken on some Caribbean islands.

Patois A simplified spoken form of a language, often French or English, which has been adapted by people in a particular region.

Population The total number of people living in a town, city, particular area, country or continent.

Pyrethrum A member of the chrysanthemum family that is used to make pesticides.

Quechua A language spoken by around 13 million people in South America. Quechua dates back to the Incas.

Rainforest A tropical forest made up of four layers –

The emergent layer: giant trees that grow above the canopy as high as 75 m.

The canopy: most of the rainforest wildlife is found in the canopy 40 m above the ground. This layer receives the most rain and sunshine so leaves, flowers and fruit grow here.

The understorey: a layer of smaller trees, climbing plants and shrubs that are able to live in the shade.

The forest floor: the ground is almost bare except for a thin layer of leaves. Very little sunlight filters down to here.

Rainforests act as global air conditioners. They absorb carbon dioxide from the air, store the carbon, and then release fresh, clean oxygen. The world loses 50 species of plants and animals every day due to rainforest deforestation – many before they have been catalogued and studied.

Range (mountains) A group of mountains.

Sea level The level of the sea's surface. It is used as the starting point for measuring the height of the surrounding land and

landforms such as hills and mountains.

Seismic waves The vibrations caused by an earthquake (the underground movement of rocks). Some waves travel at over 20,000 km/h, but can only be felt when they reach the surface.

Sisal A plant which produces a fibre suitable for making ropes and matting.

Sorghum A cereal crop widely grown in Africa. It can be used as a grain for food, and as animal feed.

Taiga The vast stretch of coniferous forest that reaches across northern Asia close to the Arctic Circle.

Taro A tropical plant with edible leaves and edible, starchy corms.

Tectonic plates The huge pieces of the Earth's crust which slot together like a jigsaw puzzle. There are oceanic plates and continental plates. The plates are constantly moving, by just a few centimetres each year, sliding and pushing against each other.

Tides The rise and then fall of the water in the world's oceans which happens twice each day. Tides are caused by the pull of the Moon's gravity. As the Earth spins and parts of its surface move past the moon, the water rises as the Moon pulls it – this is called a high tide. At the same time, parts of the Earth's surface that are not facing the Moon have a low tide.

Tropic of Cancer An imaginary line that runs around the world between the North Pole and the Equator. We use these lines to measure the Earth and to help us find places and describe different regions. The area between the Tropic of Cancer and the Tropic of Capricorn is warm and wet and is known as *the Tropics.*

Tropic of Capricorn An imaginary line that runs around the world between the South Pole and the Equator. The area between the Tropic of Capricorn and the Tropic of Cancer is warm and wet and is known as *the Tropics.*

Tundra A boggy landscape of low-growing plants and lakes that form over permafrost – a layer of permanently frozen soil found beneath the surface of many cold areas.

INDEX

MAP INDEX AND GRID REFERENCES